# MULTI-MEDIA WORSHIP:

## A MODEL AND NINE VIEWPOINTS

Edited by Myron B. Bloy, Jr.

THE SEABURY PRESS  NEW YORK

ACKNOWLEDGMENTS

Grateful acknowledgment is made to the custodian of the Standard Book of
Common Prayer and the Church Pension Fund for permission to reproduce
here the trial Liturgy of the Lord's Supper (copyright 1967). Acknowledgment is also made to Andrew Sacks, who took the photographs which appear on pages 17-50.

# CONTENTS

*Editor's Introduction*
Myron B. Bloy, Jr.                                    5

Part One: The Model

*What Is Communion?*                                 11
J. D. Burke

THE SERVICE                                          17

Part Two: Viewpoints

*The Dynamics of Worship*                            53
Robert N. Bellah

*Reflections on Liturgical Form and Function*        62
David F. K. Steindl-Rast

*The Lord's Song in a Strange Land*                  75
Harvey H. Guthrie, Jr.

*Worship as Celebration and Confrontation*           86
Howard Moody

*Worship as Revolution*                              98
Sandra Archer

*A Wedding Masque for Lonely Travelers* 104
Nancy Willard Lindbloom

*Worship: Marriage of Head and Heart* 115
Dominic L. Cirincione

*Spontaneity in Worship* 126
Gilbert H. Caldwell

*Emotional Resonance and Life Change in Worship* 133
Tony Stoneburner

# EDITOR'S INTRODUCTION

AN IMPORTANT FEATURE of our youth culture's search for new meaning and authentic life style is the underground religious quest. The signs of this quest are easy to see: courses in religion are most popular on a growing number of campuses; activist demonstrations and hippie be-ins have become for young people the contemporary equivalents of religious rites and celebrations; drugs are used and justified as aids to mystical experience; student "communes" are pop versions of monasteries; Jesus of Nazareth, fierce lover of the poor and embracer of life, is high in their pantheon of heroes. Students are, in short, less convinced that "God is dead" than the radical theologians are.

What is certainly dying, however, from the viewpoint of the young, is the "myth of rationalism," which has dominated higher education; the myth that the only reliable way to truth is through a morally and emotionally detached analysis of reality. The young have perceived that reality is too alive and demanding, its depths too mysterious and awesome, to be plumbed by such a limited instrument. This limitation is not true of Christian symbols and experience, which could be immensely important to them in their quest.

But the churches, by and large, have failed or been unable to respond effectively to the quest of the young. Most parishes and campus ministry centers appeal only to a few dependent hangers-on among youth, and no religious activity seems to be less relevant than the event of worship itself. That is why it is significant when, on a campus, worship again becomes a dynamic event engaging the imagination and participation of morally and esthetically sensitive students. One place where this new trend has been evident, where the religious quest of students finds response in the church's worship, is Canterbury House at the University of Michigan in Ann Arbor. There, in a coffeehouse that was once a printing plant, Episcopal Chaplain Daniel Burke and his growing congregation of students and faculty meet Sunday mornings to worship God in terms of *both* the Episcopal rite of Holy Communion *and* the moral and esthetic expressions of youth's religious quest. Despite whatever liturgical or esthetic shortcomings there may be, the service is clearly an *event* that stirs the hearts and minds of the new generation.

In order to help other congregations, especially campus congregations, learn from the liturgical experience of Canterbury House, the Church Society for College Work invited to Ann Arbor a group of scholars, religious leaders, and artists to discuss together the question of functions and forms of worship for man today, then to participate in the Canterbury House worship and, finally, on the basis of their discussion and experience, to write about it.

Part One of this book attempts to re-create, through photographs and short descriptive commentary on the pages opposite the service text, the worship experience that the seminar members shared that Sunday morning. In Part Two the reader will find the group's papers. The parts together constitute a case study in experimental worship that should help other congregations to discover how to enrich their own worship and to respond more effectively to the religious quest of their younger members.

To conclude this introduction and set the stage for what follows, we present the report of the service by student Jeremy Hewes, which appeared a few days later (October 25, 1968) in *The Michigan Daily:*

Communication is to, from, and among people. To succeed, it must also be of people. That is, any form of communication—sound, print, touch, whatever—must be stated in terms that people will understand and ultimately accept. These criteria likewise apply to communication of any message or set of values.

A fine example of such communication may be seen any Sunday morning at Canterbury House. A folk mass to, from, and among people is celebrated there each week. Last Sunday, the folk mass was enriched by members of the San Francisco Mime Troupe and the first showing of a film by Craig Hammond, one of the two Episcopal ministers who direct the center.

The service was a mixed-media exercise. A folk trio of Bob Franke on guitar, Gene Barkin, electric guitar, and Andy Stein, bass, accompanied the singing of formal parts of the mass and folk counterparts of hymns or anthems. In one scene, the Mime Troupe moved to the rhythm of one drum and a brief narration from *Time* magazine about prosecution of the Catonsville nine [a Catholic group that destroyed some draft files in a war protest]; in another, a "cranky" of rolled paper illustrated the tale of a soldier told by an actor and punctuated by two recorders. The color film combined an excellent spatial collage for an episode with the people themselves and their best communicators, children. A musical track accompanied the film, introduced by the Beatles singing "Fool on the Hill."

Yet the litany of the mass was not abandoned. Martin Bell and Bob Franke have written music for the Kyrie, Creed, Agnus Dei, and other elements of the mass. The people, performers, and celebrants sang together. Message, too, was in the singing—as in a verse of Franke's "Pilgrimage":

> For doubt drove us down as
> we walked upon the road
> And a rain of indifference
> held us back

And the maps of your mystery
weren't noticed by the blind
When fear turned the day—
light black.

Hammond read the epistle to the trio's quiet playing and humming of "Hey Jude," and people were asked to participate in the
prayer of intercession. One man said, "Prayer is so often a downer,
I pray it would be otherwise." And communion was celebrated
with round loaves of bread in baskets, and wine in earthenware gob-
lets passed among the people.

The focus was constantly shifting and the scene changing during
the service, but nothing seemed to be forced upon the people—
things were being done their way and the points were made. Dan
Burke, the minister who officiated at the folk mass, was silent for
a moment after the gospel was read, then he said, "You can hardly
avoid it, but touch each other." Then louder, "Come on, touch
each other." Two hundred and fifty people sat on the floor and
the stage, leaned against walls and railings, hand in hand. Communication became fellowship—the message was the people, and,
if only for a few moments or a few hours, the message was lived.

# PART ONE:

---

# THE MODEL

On the pages opposite the text of the service (pp. 17-50) are photographs and brief descriptions of the actions taking place at specific points in the service.

# WHAT IS COMMUNION?

## by J. D. Burke

To BEGIN at the beginning, the Bible is an unambiguous and unconditional assertion that everyone and everything is in communion—just as is. To be sure ambiguity sets in almost immediately, and is closely followed by ambivalence—all of which is finally sealed by dichotomization. But, in the words of the Sunday school teacher, "the Bible tells us" that first of all there is Paradise or the Kingdom of God. As it were, this is how it all started, this is how every moment starts, and there is the clear implication that this is how it all will end. In the meantime we are warned not to eat the apple of dichotomy. So far from crowning all knowledge, its effect is fatal. The tree is there (here) in the garden, obviously. It isn't that Yes-Yeses and No-Nos have no meaning or place, but it literally makes a world of difference whether one views them as points on a continuum or different categories of being. The result of this vital difference is just what the Genesis legend says: It is life or death.

Communion. This assertion—one might call it an assumption, a hypothesis, or even a blik—provides the ground on which one then moves into the world ambience, living it as a greater or less realization of this basic theme. It might be laboring the obvious, but it should be pointed out that this basic assumption of wholeness is not the starting point for much that passes itself off as religious, whether Christian or otherwise. And even when it is, it is immediately so qualified and disqualified by human ambivalence that it quickly becomes lost from view or pushed into another realm of experience. As a result, the starting point for comprehending our experience is dualistic, not to say schizophrenic—which, ironically, we call healthy. The universe is split into two parts and our choices are limited to some variations or amalgamations of the penultimate either/or, which, as already noted, become for us different categories of being. To name a few of the categories deemed antithetical in both conventional and sophisticated myth and wisdom, we have: sacred/secular; temporal/eternal; right/wrong; pain/pleasure; spiritual/material; transcendent/immanent; light/darkness. The list could go on and on. The most persuasive dichotomy is that all is good/evil leading to salvation/damnation. Tribalism is not the most serious obstacle to our experience of union. It is but a subset of the above.

Therefore all myth and ritual about the brotherhood of man, noble as it is, has to degenerate shortly into well-meaning blather; it is only half of the story. The gospel myth demands the larger scope which views life as some aspect of fulfillment of the brotherhood of man in the Paradise of God. It is for and against this word that we fashioned our identity. Albert Schweitzer was right. Either Jesus was a crazy, talking all that apocalyptic nonsense, or he was really talking about the whole shot. It is here that the crucial either/or resides. And it is indeed a crucial either/or for us existentially or historically despite its dissolution in the universal Yes. As a friend of mine puts it, "The thing is liking what you get as well as getting what you like."

Back to the beginning—communion. That is what worship does and is. It takes us to the beginning, to declare our communion with and in ourselves, each other, and God. It is or should be a statement—reminder of our unconditional acceptability which cuts through the befuddlement of our prerequisites.

The ways of declaring this union or telling this story in worship are manifold. Those of us in the Christian dispensation are wont to say that we perceive this abstraction concretized in the history of (old and new) Israel and with particular clarity in Jesus. We take our bearings from Jesus and Israel in worship and try to move on from there. If such concentration on Jesus and Israel as *sine qua non* of worship seems too particularized, we can only say that experience has taught us that we would be quite lost without the concreteness that Jesus and Israel offer. However, we must say also that their meaning is, in the long run, virtually useless unless it is related to both people and history in general. Not to add *that* is to compound the fatal flaw of separating sacred and secular, to tear apart once more the fabric of our basic experience of wholeness. To say, in other words, that the gospel is embodied in Jesus in particular is not to say that it is embodied in him exclusively. "Not bound by the law of logical alternatives" (as Bonhoeffer puts it), Jesus himself dealt with people as basically whole and recognized confirmations of the gospel in unlikely places. The fact that he needed to be jogged in the encounter with the Syro-Phoenician woman gives ample testimony to the power of the human tendency to be exclusive, but it also confirms the notion that truth is never partial.

Confining ourselves here to the topic of worship, it would appear then that a Christian ritual is most fully comprehended as communion when it is seen as that which is particular but not partial. No set ritual is ever going to contain this as we have had to learn to our dismay over the centuries. What McLuhan has discovered is as devastating as it may be accurate. Ritual as a thing in itself is all-pervasive. I would contend, rather, that the best thing a ritual can do for us is to remind us of that which is at the root of every experience. The fewer the links, the more poverty-stricken the ritual. Moreover, the job of ritual is only partially done if it arrests at the level of symbol or subconsciousness. The stunning failures of rationality are not going to be cured by some sort of Hegelian countertrend to formless archetype. We live in a life which takes shapes, gives utterances, and makes impingements. Sometimes the only way to handle all of this is on the symbolic level. But if it is true that nothing is so hidden that it cannot be made known, then the move is to consciousness. Worship, while dealing on all levels, should abet this movement.

Our problem, as everybody is beginning to realize, is not that there is no room or purpose for ritual in life. The problem in its most important sense is not even the question of which ritual. The problem is what, in the last analysis, is the ritual saying? Does it speak of universal wholeness or universal division? It is the fact that we speak of the latter all too often that eventually drives people away from the Good News and from the worship which is intended to give it utterance. Growth is made to precede acceptance, conditions are made to precede participation, and the net effect is to divide ourselves into in-group and out-group. The sense of unity is fractured from the start. After the glow of well-being from identity with the in-group wears off or is tested by events, the break begins to show. It makes prophets of some, but aliens of all who demur. Out of all this, sooner or later the question that is very much with us today is bound to arise—Reform or revolution? Bingo! Same old can of worms sitting on dead center. The real question still remains—Of what will you speak, union or division? The gospel, so we are persuaded, speaks of union.

All of the foregoing is a short tour de force which serves as rationale for the kinds of worship services held at Canterbury House in Ann Arbor. They are as open as we can make them while continuing to rely on the particular or concrete revelation which gave rise to Christianity. Specifically, we use the revised communion service of the Episcopal Church, identified formally as the Liturgy of the Lord's Supper, as the basic vehicle. To this may be added as many (or few) and as varied expressions of sense communication as the given situation seems to call for. The common thread that we try to keep in mind from the gospel is the verb *to commune*, common both to communion and communication.

Perhaps the first thing that might be said about worship at Canterbury House is this. It takes place in the same room where, on other occasions, we might have Odetta or the San Francisco Mime Troupe performing in the coffeehouse. Or the same room which serves betimes as a hotel for transient students. Or the same room where Jack and Marilyn have lunch weekdays at the soup kitchen. Or the same room where SDS shows *Hasta La Victoria Siempre*. Or the same room where people decide to get married, to split, where people steal money and a Buddhist monk reads his poetry, where people dance, where the black militant celebrates the July, 1967, Detroit rebellion and a Jewess cries when she is over-whelmed by a re-presentation of the holocaust.

This all in itself would not seem entirely unusual even if it suggested somehow that the distinction between sacred and secular is a figment. What may be a little out of the ordinary is the attempt we make to incorporate as many of these same people and events as we can into the worship experience. It is one thing to see the Alain Resnais film *Night and Fog*— which is a devastating muse on the concentration-camp syn-drome in human affairs—and be deeply moved by it. It is another thing to pair this with a service of Holy Communion and then try to make sense out of things like thanksgiving and forgiveness.

Juxtaposition, confrontation, and contradiction have to be

faced up to in ritual as in life. The gospel is not balm for Pollyannas or a whitewash for the Passion. It is a framework within which there is promise that the struggle can make sense. Actually, none of this is new to the liturgy itself. Perhaps that is why we have found that it is a tremendously creative springboard for contemporary expressions of contemporary issues, even with or despite its occasional obscurities, petrifactions, partialities, and misleading statements. The power of the liturgy comes from its basic intention to convey, in symbolic and rational terms, the message and experience of belonging. The power is still there, even in backfire, when, in answer to the demands of what seems like basic logic, we equivocate with ritual and make it say that only some belong or that such an experience is not a live option in this world. "In, but not of" is the name of the New Testament game which corresponds with what is implicit, at least, in the story of the Garden. We have to take both sides of the "in, but not of" seriously if we want to convey the sense of wholeness.

It is not implied, nor should it be interpreted, that what we are doing is the only, or the definitive, or *the new* way in which liturgy will have to be done. The point we would like to make is that there is a tremendous variety of ways in which the Good News can be transmitted through a traditional form. We keep trying to publish the news of God's declared communion in as sundry ways and diverse manners as we have been able to discover or excite. Acknowledging, as we do, the various and often noninstitutional ways in which this is perceived and acted out, we have been given a share in some rich experiences involving many and disparate people. We might, in the end, be rejected by all. But we hope also that there might be more moments when the gospel is perceived by all.

# THE SERVICE

## PROCESSIONAL: "PILGRIMAGE"

(Written and accompanied on acoustic guitar by Bob Franke, with back-up by electric guitar and bass. This was the accompaniment for all live music during the service, except the round at the end.)

Dear God, we have come to your table once again,
As weary and dark as the night.
We long to consume all the beauty of your love,
And to drink of your morning light.

For doubt drove us down as we walked upon the road,
And a rain of indifference held us back;
And the maps of your mystery weren't noticed by the blind
When fear turned the daylight black.

And many fell down as we walked upon the way,
For the world mixes truth with its lies;
And some of us were beaten till we couldn't understand
That the light of the world is in your eyes.

We come, now we come, to a place upon the road,
Where the hearts of the dead are reborn;
And the poverty of men sees your treasure once again,
A diamond in a crown of thorns.

Opening Versicle and Response by the Priest, the Rev. Daniel Burke, and People.

"A Son Says Goodbye to his Mother"—a Cranky done by the San Francisco Mime Troupe.

Collect led by the Priest.

# The Liturgy of the Lord's Supper

## THE CELEBRATION OF HOLY EUCHARIST
## AND MINISTRATION OF HOLY COMMUNION

A Psalm or Hymn may be sung during the Entrance of the Ministers.
The Priest or Minister appointed shall say,

BLESSED BE GOD: Father, Son, and Holy Spirit.

People

*And blessed be his Kingdom, now and forever. Amen.*

Priest

ALMIGHTY GOD, unto whom all hearts are open, all desires
known, and from whom no secrets are hid: Cleanse the
thoughts of our hearts by the inspiration of thy Holy Spirit,
that we may perfectly love thee, and worthily magnify thy
holy Name; through Christ our Lord. *Amen.*

Priest or Deacon

OUR LORD JESUS CHRIST SAYS,
The first commandment is this:
   "Hear, O Israel: The Lord our God is one Lord; and you
   shall love the Lord your God with all your heart, and
   with all your mind, and with all your strength."
The second is like it,
   "You shall love your neighbor as yourself."
There is no other commandment greater than these. On
these two commandments depend all the Law and the
Prophets.

Then this Hymn may be sung or said,

> Kyrie eleison.
> *Christe eleison.*
> Kyrie eleison.

or,

> Lord, have mercy upon us.
> *Christ, have mercy upon us.*
> Lord, have mercy upon us.

or this,

> Holy God, Holy Mighty, Holy Immortal,
> *Have mercy upon us.*

Summary of the Law, led by the Priest.

Kyrie, sung to the music of Martin Bell.

## TELEPHONE POLE SONG
(Music by Bob Franke. Sung by the People in place of the Gloria.)


You came and you asked me to be your friend;
I didn't know what you meant just then,
And now you come around and you ask me once again,
And it's not very fair to take me God knows where,
But I'll go, yes I will, yes I will.

You tell me to go into your telephone booth;
Put on the clothing of the loving eyes of youth,
And I'll come out in glory with the power of the truth,
But you tell me that I can, so I will.

You come and you ask me to give you my soul;
You pick it up broken and you give it back whole,
But I'm supposed to spend my life on your telephone pole,
And you keep telling me it's the only way to be,
And I've got to be crazy, but I will.

You tell me to love everybody alive;
I make up my list and I count about five,
But you steal my dark glasses and you take me for a drive,
And the millions that I see are all crying out to me,
And they need what I can give them, so I will.

Here, when appointed, shall be sung or said the Hymn,

### GLORIA IN EXCELSIS

GLORY BE TO GOD ON HIGH:
　　and on earth peace, good will towards men.
We praise thee, we bless thee, we worship thee,
　　we glorify thee, we give thanks to thee for thy great glory.
O Lord God, heavenly King, God the Father Almighty.

O LORD, the only-begotten Son, Jesus Christ:
O Lord God, Lamb of God, Son of the Father,
　　who takest away the sin of the world,
　　have mercy upon us.
Thou who takest away the sin of the world,
　　receive our prayer.
Thou who sittest at the right hand of God the Father,
　　have mercy upon us.

FOR THOU only art holy,
Thou only art the Lord.
Thou only, O Jesus Christ, with the Holy Spirit,
　　art most high in the glory of God the Father. Amen.

or the Hymn,

### TE DEUM LAUDAMUS

# THE MINISTRY OF THE WORD

Then the Priest shall say,

> The Lord be with you.
> *And with your spirit.*
> Let us pray.

## THE COLLECT

The People shall be seated for the following Lessons.

## THE OLD TESTAMENT LESSON

## THE EPISTLE

The person who reads the Lesson (if there be one appointed) and the Epistle shall stand in a pulpit or some other suitable place, and face the People, first saying,

> The Word of God,
> written in the Book of _____

or,

> written in the Epistle _____

After the Lesson and after the Epistle, a Psalm or Hymn may be sung.

Collect for the 19th Sunday after Trinity, read by the Priest

Old Testament reading: Job 24:1-17, translated by James Brugh, and read alternately in Hebrew and English by James Brugh and the Priest.

Epistle: Ephesians 4:1-17 (Jerusalem Bible translation), read by the Rev. Craig Hammond, with people humming the Beatles' "Hey Jude" as a background.

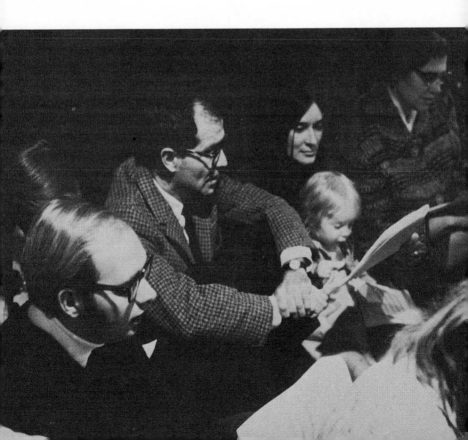

Gospel: Matthew 9:1-8 (Authorized Version in the Book of Common Prayer), read from among the People by the Rev. Gilbert Caldwell.

The Peace, given by the People, sitting on the floor, linked and swaying in rhythm with the music.

The Creed, led by the Priest, the People standing.

## The Gospel

Then, all the People standing, the Deacon (or a Priest) shall face the People and read the Gospel from a pulpit or some other suitable place, first saying,

The Holy Gospel of our Lord and Saviour Jesus Christ, according to Saint _____

And the People shall say,

Glory be to thee, O Lord.

After the Gospel, the People shall say,

Praise be to thee, O Christ.

Then follows

## The Sermon

On all Sundays and festivals, there follows, the People standing,

## The Nicene Creed

WE BELIEVE IN ONE GOD
the Father Almighty, Maker of heaven and earth, and of all things visible and invisible.

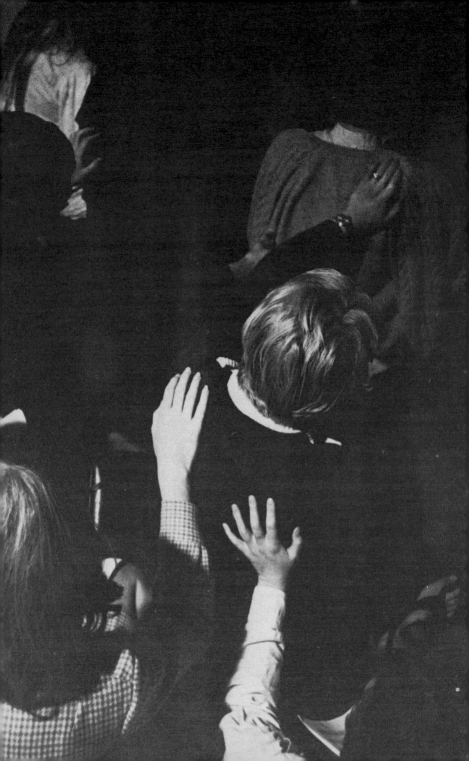

And in one Lord, Jesus Christ,
    the only-begotten Son of God,
    begotten of the Father before all worlds:
God, of God: Light, of Light: Very God, of very God:
    begotten, not made,
    being of one substance with the Father,
    and through whom all things were made:
Who for us men and for our salvation came down from
      heaven,
    and was incarnate by the Holy Spirit of the Virgin Mary,
    and was made man:
And was crucified also for us under Pontius Pilate;
    he suffered and was buried:
And the third day he rose again
    in accordance with the Scriptures:
And ascended into heaven,
    and is seated at the right hand of the Father:
And he shall come again, with glory,
    to judge both the living and the dead;
    his kingdom shall have no end.

And we believe in the Holy Spirit, the Lord:
    The Giver of Life,
    proceeding from the Father:
Who with the Father and the Son together
    is worshipped and glorified;
    who spoke by the Prophets.
And we believe in one holy Catholic and Apostolic Church:
We acknowledge one Baptism for the remission of sins:
And we look for the resurrection of the dead,
    and the life of the world to come. Amen.

Prayer of Intercession, led by two students reading alternate intercessions; grounded by a member of the congregation who offered the petition that the prayer not continue to be such a "down experience."

Here on occasions, and as appointed, follows

## The Penitential Order
(see pages 21–22)


Then the Priest and People shall exchange one with another

## The Peace

The Peace of the Lord be always with you.
*And with your spirit.*


After which, the Deacon or Priest, or some other person appointed, shall lead the People in

## The Prayer of Intercession

In PEACE, let us pray to the Lord:
For the peace from above, for the salvation of mankind: that righteousness, mercy, and truth may prevail among all peoples and nations,
*Hear us, good Lord.*

For the well-being of thy holy Catholic Church in every place: that thou wilt confirm it in the truth of thy holy Word, and grant to all Christians to live in unity, love, and concord,
*Hear us, good Lord.*

For Bishops and other Ministers, especially for N., our Presiding Bishop, N (N)., our Bishop (s), and those who serve thee in this place: that both by their life and teaching, they may set forth thy true and life-giving Word, and faithfully administer thy holy Sacraments,
*Hear us, good Lord.*

For all who bear authority in this and every land, and especially for the President of the United States [*or*, of this Nation]: that in thy holy fear they may govern the peoples in wisdom, justice, and peace,
*Hear us, good Lord.*

For all who spread the Gospel among the nations, and who minister to the suffering, the friendless, and the needy: that they may have strength and courage to fulfill thy holy will,
*Hear us, good Lord.*

For all who labor in commerce and industry, especially those whose work is dangerous or burdensome; for all who are engaged in the arts and sciences, and those who teach and study in schools of good learning; for all who keep house and train children: that they may be worthy of their calling to serve thee and their fellow men,
*Hear us, good Lord.*

For those who farm the fields and tend the woods; for all who gather the harvest of the lands and of the waters; and for our faithful use of thy creative bounty: that mankind, being delivered from famine and disaster, may acknowledge thy glory in all thy works,
*Hear us, good Lord.*

[Here may be inserted any particular bidding, according to times and occasions, or at the special request of the Congregation.

For _____, and more especially _____:
that *they* may _____, according to thy will,
        *Hear us, good Lord.*]

For all who in this transitory life are in danger, trouble, sorrow, need, sickness, or any other adversity [and especially for thy servants NN.]: that they may have comfort and relief according to their necessities,
        *Hear us, good Lord.*

For all thy people, and especially those who worship in this place: that with faith, reverence, and godly fear, they may serve thee with a glad mind and ready will all the days of their life,
        *Hear us, good Lord.*

Have mercy upon us, most merciful Lord, and deliver us from all affliction, strife, and catastrophe: in thy compassion forgive us all our sins and failures, known and unknown, things done and left undone: and so uphold us by thy Spirit, that we may end our days in peace, trusting in thy mercy at the day of judgment,
        *Have mercy upon us.*

We commend to thy keeping all thy servants departed this life in thy faith and fear [and especially thy servant (s), N (N).]: that thou wilt grant them mercy, light, and peace. May we with all thy saints [and especially N., whose faith and devotion we commemorate this day], be partakers of thine everlasting kingdom: through the mercies and merits of thy Son, Jesus Christ, our only Mediator and Advocate.

*To thee be honor, glory, and dominion, now and forever. Amen.*

If there is no Communion, all that is before appointed may be said, concluding with THE LORD'S PRAYER and THE GRACE.

# THE OFFERTORY

The Priest shall go to the Holy Table and begin THE OFFERTORY as follows, the People standing.

LET US WITH GLADNESS present the offerings and oblations of our life and labor unto the Lord.

The Priest may read one or more of the Offertory Sentences. (See pages 23–24.)

Representatives of the Congregation shall receive the alms and other offerings of the People. Both the alms and the oblations of bread and wine shall be brought to the Deacon or Priest. The Priest shall present and offer the alms and oblations, and place them upon the Holy Table, the People standing.

Offertory accompanied by the showing of an 8mm film by Craig Hammond, with the Beatles' "Fool on the Hill" and "Flying" as sound track.

Sursum Corda, Preface, Sanctus, Benedictus, sung by the People to the music of Martin Bell.

One of the following Sentences may be said or sung at

## THE PRESENTATION

Thine, O Lord, is the greatness, and the power, and the glory, and the victory, and the majesty:
*For all that is in the heaven and in the earth is thine.*
Thine is the kingdom, O Lord,
*And thou art exalted as head above all.*

or this,

All things come of thee, O Lord:
*And of thine own have we given thee.*

or this,

Worthy art thou, our Lord and God, to receive glory and honor and power,
*For thou hast created all things, and by thy will they exist and were created.*


## THE CONSECRATION

The Priest shall face the People, still standing, and shall sing or say,

The Lord be with you.
*And with your spirit.*

LIFT UP your hearts.
*We lift them up unto the Lord.*
Let us give thanks unto our Lord God.
*It is meet and right so to do.*

IT IS TRULY MEET, right, and our bounden duty, that we should at all times and in all places, give thanks unto thee, O Lord, Holy Father, Almighty, Everlasting God:

Through Jesus Christ our Lord, who on On Sundays this day overcame death and the grave, and by his glorious resurrection opened to us the way of everlasting life:

Or the Proper Preface, as appointed (pages 25–29):

THEREFORE with Angels and Archangels, and with all the company of heaven, we laud and magnify thy glorious Name, evermore praising thee and saying,

### Priest and People

HOLY, HOLY, HOLY, Lord God of Hosts: Heaven and earth are full of thy glory. Glory be to thee, O Lord most high.

Here the People may kneel; and the Priest shall continue,

ALL GLORY BE TO THEE, Almighty God, Holy Father, Creator of heaven and earth, who didst make us in thine own image. And when we had fallen into sin, thou of thy tender mercy didst give thine only-begotten Son Jesus Christ, to take our nature upon him, and to suffer death upon the Cross for our redemption: Who made there, by his one oblation of himself once offered, a full and perfect sacrifice for the whole world: And instituted and commanded us to continue this perpetual memorial of his precious death and sacrifice, until his coming again.

"Trial of the Catonsville 9," a dramatic presentation by
the San Francisco Mime Troupe; in place of the paragraph
beginning, "All Glory be to thee."

Prayer of Consecration (beginning, "For in the night"), said first by the Priest alone, and then by the Priest and People together.

FOR IN THE NIGHT in which he was betrayed, he took bread; and when he had given thanks to thee, he broke it, and gave it to his disciples, and said, "Take, eat: This is my Body which is given for you. Do this in remembrance of me."

*Here the Priest is to lay his hands upon all the bread*

In the same way also, after supper, he took the cup; and when he had given thanks, he gave it to them and said, "Drink this, all of you: For this is my Blood of the New Covenant, which is poured out for you and many for the forgiveness of sins. Do this, as often as you drink it, in remembrance of me."

*Here he is to lay his hand upon every vessel of wine to be blessed*

WHEREFORE, O LORD AND HOLY FATHER, we thy people do celebrate here before thy Divine Majesty, with these thy holy Gifts, which we offer unto thee, the memorial of the blessed Passion and precious Death of thy dear Son, his mighty Resurrection and glorious Ascension, looking for his Coming again in power and great glory. And herewith we offer and present unto thee, O Lord, ourselves, which is our bounden duty and service. And we entirely desire thy fatherly goodness mercifully to accept, through the eternal mediation of our Saviour Jesus Christ, this our sacrifice of praise and thanksgiving.

WE PRAY THEE, GRACIOUS FATHER, of thine almighty power, to bless and sanctify us and these holy Mysteries with thy Life-giving Word and Holy Spirit. Fill with thy grace all who partake of the Body and Blood of our Lord Jesus Christ. Make us one Body, that he may dwell in us and we in him.

And grant that with boldness we may confess thy Name in constancy of faith, and at the last Day enter with all thy saints into the joy of thine eternal kingdom:

Through the same Jesus Christ our Lord; by whom, and with whom, and in whom, in the unity of the Holy Spirit, all honor and glory be unto thee, O Father Almighty, world without end.

AMEN.

As our Saviour Christ has taught us, we are now bold to say:

Priest and People

OUR FATHER, who art in heaven, Hallowed be thy Name. Thy kingdom come. Thy will be done, On earth as it is in heaven. Give us this day our daily bread. And forgive us our trespasses, As we forgive those who trespass against us. And lead us not into temptation; But deliver us from evil. For thine is the kingdom, and the power, and the glory, for ever and ever. Amen.

# THE BREAKING OF THE BREAD

Here the Priest shall break the consecrated Bread, and silence shall be kept for a space.

Then shall be said or sung the following Anthem, or some other proper Hymn. From Easter Day to Trinity Sunday,

Alleluia

may be sung or said before and after the Anthem.

The Lord's Prayer, sung by the People to the music of Martin Bell.

Agnus Dei, sung by the People to the music of Martin Bell.

Administration of the Bread and Wine: loaves of bread broken into large pieces and passed by the celebrant and his assistant among congregation, which in turn passed it around. Wine bottles passed around by congregation. Music background was the singing of "Hey Jude" with instrumental accompaniment.

CHRIST OUR PASSOVER is sacrificed for us:
*Therefore let us keep the feast.*

Blessed is He who comes in the Name of the Lord.
*Hosanna in the highest.*

Then the Priest shall face the People and say,

HOLY THINGS for the People of God: Take them in remembrance that Christ gives himself for you, and feed on him in your hearts by faith, with thanksgiving.

The Minister who delivers the Bread shall say,

THE BODY of our Lord Jesus Christ keep you unto everlasting life.

The Minister who delivers the Cup shall say:

THE BLOOD of our Lord Jesus Christ keep you unto everlasting life.

Opportunity shall always be given to every communicant to receive the consecrated Bread and Wine separately. But the Sacrament may be received in both kinds simultaneously, in such manner as is authorized by the Ordinary, in which case the Minister shall say,

THE BODY AND BLOOD of our Lord Jesus Christ keep you unto everlasting life.

When all have communicated, the Priest shall say,

## Let us give thanks to the Lord.

*Priest and People*

ALMIGHTY AND EVERLIVING GOD, we most heartily thank thee, That thou dost feed us in these holy Mysteries, With the spiritual food of the most precious Body and Blood of our Saviour Jesus Christ, Assuring us thereby of thy favor and goodness towards us; And that we are truly members incorporate in the mystical Body of thy Son, The blessed company of all faithful people; And heirs, through hope, of thine everlasting kingdom. And we humbly pray thee, O heavenly Father, so to assist us by thy Holy Spirit, That we may continue in that holy fellowship, And do all such good works as thou hast prepared for us; Through Jesus Christ our Lord, To whom, with thee and the same Spirit, be all honor and glory, world without end. Amen.

Then shall the Priest or Deacon dismiss the People as follows. But if the Bishop is present, he shall dismiss the People and give them his blessing.

GO FORTH INTO THE WORLD IN PEACE. Be strong and of good courage. Hold fast that which is good. Love and serve the Lord with gladness and singleness of heart, rejoicing in the power of his Spirit. *Amen.*

Thanksgiving: A round sung by members of the San Francisco Mime Troupe, first among themselves, and then with the People at their request.

The Benediction: The single word "Peace" spoken by the Priest as he gave the hand signal for Peace, which the People returned.

Postlude: Spontaneous jam of rock music by the musicians (some from the congregation, some from the Mime Troupe, along with scheduled morning musicians) with the people dancing and/or drinking coffee.

# PART TWO:

---

# VIEWPOINTS

# THE DYNAMICS OF WORSHIP

## by Robert N. Bellah

*Robert N. Bellah, of the University of California at Berkeley, is a leading sociologist of religion. When the group gathered to discuss the functions and forms of worship for man today, Bellah led off by arguing (as he does in the following paper) that the function of worship is to help men break through the "straight, or profane, world of everyday pragmatic common sense" in order to facilitate the experience of the holy. Our difficulty in accomplishing this breakthrough, he argued, defines the crisis of worship in our time.*—ED.

> *For everything that lives is Holy.*
> WILLIAM BLAKE

BLAKE'S WORDS do not really deny the contrast between sacred and profane. For the sacred is not simply a property of external objects any more than it is purely a subjective feeling. It is a quality of experience, of relation between subject and object. The apprehension that everything that lives is holy does not arise from sense perception, does not have in Blake's words a "Philosophic and Experimental" character. Rather, it arises from a different kind of perception which Blake called "Poetic or Prophetic." The first thing about worship, if we define it as a human activity that attempts to relate to the sacred, or holy, is that it tries to break through the straight, or profane, world of everyday pragmatic common sense.

Evidence that worship attempts to break the hold of the ordinary and the usual is the frequent conception of worship as a symbolic "trip," an identification with the travels of a hero or the journey to Golgotha, a "descent" into the depths, the caves of mystery, or an "ascent" to the realms of light "above." At any rate there is a departure from the plane of the mundane, a departure which often arouses a sense of the uncanny, of the presence of the *mysterium tremendum*. A wide variety of techniques has been developed to break up the ordinary patterns of perception and allow the emergence of other dimensions of experience—rhythmic chanting, ecstatic dancing, or, more familiarly, the silence and simplicity of the Quaker meeting or the solemn orderliness of Episcopal morning prayer. It is one of the chief problems of contemporary worship that the traditional types of aesthetic manipulation do not work, do not precipitate the worshipers into a state of altered consciousness. Remaining in the state of everyday common sense they see nothing in the service but the literal, which may be instructive or not, but is very seldom religiously transformative.

There must, of course, be links between the worship service and the immediate personal and social reality of the worshipers. But even when attained, the element of "relevance," so highly regarded today, is only a shaky first step. Unless there is a link between the religious symbols making up the worship ceremony and the particular past and present of the worshipers, then the worship process cannot begin. Indeed, the more deeply the symbols do grasp the real problems and conflicts of the worshipers, the more powerful the subsequent experience can be. But what happens in worship is the transformation of the personal into the transpersonal, the immediate into the transtemporal. Through this transformation the immediate problems and conflicts can be seen in a new light, insight can be achieved and postworship changes in behavior can ensue. How we evaluate these changes, which may range from fleeing to the desert to starting a social revolution, depends on our values and is not at issue here. But the point is that the mythical, archetypal, timeless character of religious symbols provides a perspective relative to everyday reality without which, in Blake's words, the latter would "stand still unable to do other than repeat the same dull round over again."

Worship to be maximally effective must provide not only a symbolic reordering of experience but an element of consummation and fulfillment. The experience of worship should produce an influx of life and power, a feeling of wholeness, of the grace of God, of being at the still center of the turning wheel. If this happens there may occur a shift in the definition of the boundary of the self, perhaps, as with Blake, an identification with everything that lives, but at any rate a transformation of motivation, commitment, and value which may galvanize not only individuals but the collectivity of worshipers.

If worship does not "work" it may not be because it is "irrelevant." It almost certainly is not because modern man is capable of living a purely secular existence without it. A modern straight type is apt to be in the grip of powerful unconscious fantasies which repeat themselves endlessly but get nowhere. He is on a very bad trip but he doesn't know it, or he knows it only when he becomes conscious of his incipient alcoholism, his bad marriage, his unsatisfying job. It is just because he is on such a bad trip, not because he is so "mature," that he cannot let down his defenses enough to participate meaningfully in an act of worship. Worship involves a partial regression from normal defensive ego functioning, so that there is a greater openness to both inner and outer reality. But precisely this regression and this openness may be seen as dangerous and threatening to the ego. Traditionally, religious ritual has often solved this problem by itself being taken up into a compromise formation as a compulsive defense mechanism.

Worship, then, whose essential function we have argued is to facilitate the experience of the holy, can actually become a defense against that experience. If the traditional rituals often attempted to bind the power of the sacred into a compulsive pattern which acted like a neurotic symptom, the modern debasement of worship into moral edification devoid of the power of the holy is not adequate either. I would not want to exaggerate the extent to which worship is ineffective today. I think of a Catholic student of mine who, after many years of routine attendance at Mass, one Sunday completely identified with the Mass, understood for the first time what it meant, and was deeply changed by the experience. Many less dramatic examples come to mind. But the situation is sufficiently troublesome to justify the wide range of experimentation and innovation which is currently going on in this area.

The foregoing paragraphs were written before attending the worship service at Canterbury House on October 20, 1968. It is now my task to consider that service in the light of my previous views, and my views in light of the service. Anything I might say about the service is severely limited by the fact that I have the experience of only one participant, namely myself, to go on. Extensive interviews with a cross-section of those present would be necessary before one could begin to speak of what happened at the service in a way that is not biased by one's own position and idiosyncrasies.

The first thing that strikes me is the contrast in atmosphere with most services I have attended, services mainly in urban and suburban Protestant churches. Perhaps the closest approximation in my experience to the general informality and relaxation which prevailed was the Mormon meeting that I went to during several months of field work in rural New Mexico some fourteen years ago. But whereas the casual dress and crying babies reminded me of the Mormons, the sitting on the floor in a room utterly devoid of any of the qualities of a "church" pushed the atmosphere of official religion even more into the background. What seemed to be going on was not merely a relaxation of some of the stringencies of middle-class decorum, but a conscious opposition to the accepted symbolizations of what is religious. Bob Dylan's "Like a Rolling Stone," for example, which was sung quietly, almost tenderly (in contrast to Dylan's own defiant rendition), before the service began, would not normally be considered "religious" by anyone in American society.

Indeed, in a number of respects—the use of music with sexual and aggressive overtones, the coffeehouse atmosphere, the movies, the political activism of the San Francisco Mime Troupe—what was being included was not merely the religiously neutral but the consciously profane. The symbolic context of the worship was not the world of everyday, of business, of domesticity or the academic, but the worlds of teenage recreation (with its overtone of "sin") and of activist politics, two worlds as "set apart" from daily life as is the more usual conception of the religious. The elements of danger and excitement which are partially associated with these worlds helped to heighten the atmosphere of the nonordinary, to give the worship the quality of a "trip." While this venture into the outskirts of the forbidden may seem daring in contrast to the conventionalities of middle-class religiosity, it is of course quite mild compared with the frequent appearance of orgiastic behavior in religious contexts throughout the

world. Durkheim among others has pointed out the ambivalence of the sacred and how the sacrilegious can be easily,
much more easily than the religiously neutral, transformed
into its opposite.

Of course I do not mean to exaggerate the use of profane
themes. The basic structure and much of the language of
the service was provided by the Episcopal Liturgy of the
Lord's Supper with its thoroughly traditional symbolism.
However, the continuous switching between the words of the
Prayer Book and such things as "The Fool on the Hill" or
"Hey Jude" was itself a central device of the service. Presumably it served to heighten the meaning both of the biblical
language and symbols and of the consciously secular cultural
allusions and to include them in some kind of greater whole.
The form was a kaleidoscopic series of juxtaposed interludes
without any central argument to tie them together. The
sermon was conspicuously absent and the Mime Troupe performance in no way took its place. It was one fragment alongside others and not an attempt at intellectual integration. The
atmosphere of spontaneous disorganization was so complete
as to be almost contrived. Indeed, Dan Burke seemed deliberately bent on shattering any possible element of solemnity by following almost every heavily formal statement in
the liturgy with an ad lib remark in ordinary language.
Whether in fact an atmosphere of deliberate spontaneity
rather than one of contrived solemnity helps to provide a
meaningful experience of worship depends on the response of
particular worshipers. But here we can perhaps say a bit more
about the kind of experience that the Canterbury House group
was trying to convey.

On the basis of Dan Burke's paper and also of the article
in the *Michigan Daily* of October 25, 1968, by Jeremy Joan
Hewes, we can surmise that the central idea behind the serv-

ice is communion and communication. What is being asserted is that (in spite of appearances) communion is basic, all men are acceptable, and we can communicate with each other. We need not preclude the issue of meaning by restricting it to this consciously intended level—there are obviously many unconscious levels of meaning going on and the powerful symbols invoked in such a service have meanings which cannot be entirely shaped to conscious intention. But we can consider the extent to which the conscious aim may have been fulfilled, though lacking the evidence really to answer the question. For me there was a sense of spontaneous participation, though—and this may be due to my age and world-view—it was partial and flickering. Much of what happened, as in conventional services, was a performance put on by a few people for an audience of nonparticipators. This holds for the beautiful and touching movie as well as for the, to me, somewhat less effective performances by the Mime Troupe. The music and the responsive readings might have been more effective in creating a sense of participation if they had been more familiar or, in one case (the "Telephone Pole Song"), less sentimental. The moment when we were asked to touch each other and move together was somewhat artificial and strained (I consciously wanted it to work but perhaps I was too uptight). The one moment when communion became reality was the Communion itself. Perhaps here for me there was just the right admixture of the familiar and the unfamiliar. The good brown bread in the round loaves, the bottles of wine being poured into the earthenware cups really were somehow transmuted into the body and the blood, and partaking of them was to become one with the body of Christ, the body of man. In that moment the self-consciousness which I carried into the service and held on to tightly throughout most of it was broken through.

Finally, let me reconsider some of the theoretical issues of my statements in the first part of this chapter in the light of the experience of this service. Certainly one of the things the service was trying to do was to break through the usual cognitive frameworks and put things in a new perspective. This it did mainly through the radical juxtaposition of things normally considered separate, so that their fundamental unity, the reality of communion, would shine through. The service attempted as much as possible to touch upon and gather up the concerns of the worshipers, very centrally the anxieties and protests about the Vietnam war. The purpose of these references, however, was not just to moralize but to show in the midst of disruption and distortion the present reality of communion as symbolized centrally in the age-old performance of the Eucharist. Presumably the disparate cultural elements brought together in the service and transmuted into some kind of form, however loose, should provide an objective framework in terms of which the inner psychic transformation of the worshiper could take place. In the movie *Rachel, Rachel* one was shown how a worship experience, even one where it was not clear whether the experience was a good or a bad trip for the heroine, opened up entirely new life possibilities for Rachel. Our lack of access to the inner lives of the Canterbury House worshipers prevents us from knowing if any comparable transformation occurred. But that could have happened, and less drastic transformations of feeling almost certainly occurred.

But as in any human situation, the aims of this event were only partially attained. I have already touched on the problem of the failure of the worshiper "to get with it" because of his own inner blocks. Let us now consider the possible perversion of the worship ceremony itself into a defense against the experience it is supposed to embody.

The conventional service today lacks authenticity because

it has no surprises; it is not a point at which the world of everyday is broken through but only a particularly cozy corner of it. Certainly the Canterbury House service contained the possibility of opening up new ranges of experience. I could not help but feel, however, that there was an ever so slight element of exhibitionism, of deliberate shock (this is in part because the Mime Troupe clearly suffers from this problem, though not wholly from that source), in taking what is familiar in one group, namely left-wing student culture, and deliberately mixing it with traditional religion. The danger here is that the kick may come not from discovering something genuinely new oneself but from appearing *avant-garde* to others, even to others not actually present, such as parents. The clichés of student culture are no more inherently profound than the clichés of any other group. Left-wing politics can be as much an escape from reality as compulsive money-making. There is the danger, then, of simply switching from one style of culture religion to another. To the extent that the traditional religious symbols operated to call into question and not simply to validate the contemporary cultural materials in the service, the danger was avoided.

# REFLECTIONS ON LITURGICAL FORM AND FUNCTION

## by David F. K. Steindl-Rast

*David F. K. Steindl-Rast, monk of the Benedictine Mount Saviour Monastery near Elmira, New York, was in essential agreement with Bellah. Worship, in Brother David's view, is a "pushing through" into Mystery and "takes place through symbol and symbolic action." He found the coffeehouse service successful in part but also frenetic and its overall impact diffused by too many elements. Brother David received his Ph.D. degree in experimental psychology from the University of Vienna and in recent years has become a well-known student and interpreter of Zen.—*ED.

AN EARLY Vedic text calls man "the only animal capable of worship." Could "contemporary" man truly have lost this capability? And what would this mean? The implications of our topic are so far-reaching that we must build our argument on as broad a basis as possible. This chapter is indeed occasioned by one specific experimental worship service, and this particular example will serve as a point of reference; but if we want to understand the function of worship for contemporary man we must ask in the most general terms: What is the function of worship for man wherever we find it? What need has it served in man's life since prehistoric times? And if we want to find forms of worship appropriate for our time we must first inquire into the fundamental structure on which the forms of worship in all their variety have been based throughout history.

What does man seek in worship? A contemporary answer is implied in a remarkable paragraph written by a teenage member of the Unitarian Church of Ithaca, New York. Their youth group visited the Benedictine Monastery of Mount Saviour for Vespers one evening, and in the next issue of the Unitarian Church Bulletin the following lines appeared under the title "Insights":

. . . In the chapel there were only a few people watching the service, and I sat in front of them. I wanted the sensation of being alone there. I wanted to be open to the beauty of the chapel and the circle of monks and to the chanting. And I see now that I wanted more than that. I wanted through some sort of magic to enter into the service, not simply because its forms were beautiful, but because they seemed at once mysterious and full of meaning. . . . The monks knelt and rose and bowed; bowing, their bodies bent forward from the waist, torsos almost horizontal. But I could not move. This is reasonable. I was brought up in this church where no one kneels and no one bows. Physically, I'm very inhibited, so that I don't move easily. And when has it ever been suggested that I might kneel, even figuratively kneel, before or to something? I wanted to kneel, that's the important thing. But I could not. . . . To kneel and to mean it would be frightening, because there is a darkness in the kneeling and a darkness in us which we cannot reason about. You teach the fear of form without meaning, and that is right; but having avoided forms, you have sometimes avoided the darkness, and it is from the darkness that the real questions arise.

This is clearly a contemporary voice. And yet, these few lines strike three key notes of timeless importance within the context of worship: "meaning" or significance, "form" or symbol, and Mystery, "the darkness in us which we cannot reason about." An inquiry into these three areas will inevitably lead us to the very core of our topic.

From the dawn of consciousness on (and we may take this historically as well as psychologically), man experiences his world as floating on Mystery. A child's definition of the world reflects quite accurately this experience: "The world," says the child, "is so you have something to stand on." Mystery surrounds everything, but the world of familiar objects gives us at least a safe footing. And what this image implies for the child becomes clear when we hear the corresponding definition for a floor: "A floor is so you won't fall into the hole your house stands on." A profound philosophical insight lies in this childish image: the insight that we comprehend reality always as embedded in the incomprehensible.

Our term "to comprehend" comes from the Latin word *comprehendere,* which means to grasp something all around, to embrace it from all sides, to hold onto it, to have a firm grip on it. But can we really "comprehend" reality as thoroughly as that? Do not all our efforts to comprehend lead us again and again to the incomprehensible? And here we do not only mean the not-yet-understood; we mean above all the essentially incomprehensible, Mystery, which provides the foil for all human comprehension.

When we grasp something intellectually, we say: "I see"; but our seeing is always a perception of contrast. White chalk will write legibly on a blackboard, not on the white wall. In the same way we grasp by contrast to a background of reality which we cannot grasp, call it the incomprehensible Ground of Being, "the darkness in us which we cannot reason about," or simply Mystery. Man has no choice: he must relate his world to Mystery. And in this relation he discovers something new: meaning. With the first "Why?" a child asks, he has set out on a lifelong quest for meaning. Man finds himself surrounded by a world of things and events, and not only surrounded by it, but deeply immersed and intimately interwoven in it. And yet, man "sticks out" of this world of things and events. This is, after all, what it means to exist. *Existere* means literally "to stick out." Have we not all experienced how we protrude over the surface of the world around us, even though sometimes we would rather be submerged? In spite of ourselves we stick out. And we do so because we ask questions. We stick out into the realm of meaning because we are the animals who ask "Why?"

"Why?" is the key the small child uses incessantly, trying to open the doors of reality. Man's consciousness becomes truly human at the moment he realizes that things need not be what they are, and, in fact, that they need not be at all. This is what his "Why?" implies; this is why he will not cease to use this key until he reaches the realm of Mystery. It is in this openness toward Mystery that he "exists" as man. Be it like an open door or like an open wound, the heart of man is that point of the world which is open toward Mystery.

Man is open, but merely as an open question. He asks for meaning. Man is the one animal who asks this question. He asks for the significance of things, and does not cease until he comes to ask for their ultimate significance. But in asking for the ultimate meaning of the world, man questions the significance of his own existence. All that he is culminates in this questioning. I am a human being, and so I am an open question. But from where shall I expect an answer? Within the given framework of the world I might succeed in finding a place for myself without transcendent reference. But when I come to ask for the significance of the world as a whole, the answer must lie beyond it, in the realm of its incomprehensible ground which we called "Mystery."

If I am an open question, I cannot give meaning to myself; I must receive it. But from where shall I receive it, if not from the realm of Mystery? Hence it will not be an answer which removes Mystery: the ultimate answer must leave Mystery intact and yet be an answer. It will be paradoxical also in this way: I will not be able to take and have this answer once and for all; I will have to receive it anew, again and again. It is the light that makes us discern things; and yet, we cannot take and have light in the way in which things can be taken and had. Neither light nor meaning can be had "for keeps." Both must constantly be received from their source. Mystery is the source of that lightless light in which alone man can discern a meaning that will satisfy his heart.

"Heart," as we are using the term here, is not a synonym for man's emotional life. By "heart" we mean what the lover means who desires the heart of the beloved. And since "heart" in this sense is the "root of my being"—where intellect, will, and emotions are still one—the encounter with meaning cannot be a purely intellectual matter. It concerns the whole man. Nothing can become meaningful to me unless my will is involved together with my intellect, and my emotions too. The heart is that core and center where I am most intimately myself and, at the same time, most intimately united with the whole human community. It is this innermost heart of man which alone perceives the deepest significance of things and events: man's heart is the "organ" for meaning.

Meaning, as we conceive it here, stands in a relation of tension (though not in opposition) to purpose. It can become a frightening discovery for any one of us that there is purposeful activity which may, nevertheless, be without meaning. Suddenly a man may become aware: "My life is filled with a thousand purposes, but it isn't really a meaningful life." Purpose always leads to another purpose, and we deceive ourselves if we think that meaning can be the end-station of that railroad line of which each stop is another in-order-to. There is no end-station to the railway of purpose; it goes on and on endlessly. Meaning is wherever you get off.

"Getting off" means finding the one activity which has all

its in-order-to within itself, and that is celebration. But we shouldn't call it an "activity"; it is an attitude. Celebration is that attitude which makes any activity meaningful by giving it that margin of leisure in which the heart can rest and find meaning. Leisure, thus understood, is not "time off." Leisure is an inner distance from work as well as from rest, a detachment that creates space around everything, space and silence in which things and events can come to themselves and reveal their meaning.

In whatever man does, he is motivated by both purpose and meaning. To sustain his existence as man he simply needs more meaning than mere purpose can hold. From the dawn of time, therefore, man gave to the things that serve his purpose a meaning which goes far beyond that purpose. The striking of fire, the bath, the meal—every action of daily life is charged with cosmic significance for primitive man, and so is the layout of his dwellings, the adornment of his body, the shape of his tools and all things he makes. Even our civilization, so far removed from the source, tries to give to things a meaning that goes beyond purpose, by making them at least status symbols, status being the last remnant of an immaterial reality embodied in material things.

Symbol and "embodiment" belong closely together in our context. For when we say "symbol" we mean a sign that contains and embodies the meaning to which it points. We are familiar with this kind of symbol through our own existence in the body. Man has symbols only because he is a symbol. He discovers the paradox of the symbol in his own heart. He realizes that his appearance in the world embodies the meaning of his life, without being able to exhaust this meaning. My appearance (both in the sense of my stepping onto the stage of the world, and in the sense of the mask I wear) is the manifestation and realization of my heart. But the heart is inexhaustible. It has a share in "the darkness in us which we cannot reason about." Man discovers himself as symbol when he becomes aware that in his life Mystery comes to itself and reveals its meaning.

Man is the animal that has symbols because he is open toward Mystery, points toward Mystery, embodies Mystery. Man is a symbol for Mystery. He points to a reality with which he communicates in his intimate depth, although he is infinitely far from being identical with it. He receives his meaning from beyond himself, and so he must freely open himself to receive this meaning, or become absurd. Man is the symbol which is bound in freedom to become more and more transparent for his own true meaning. He is free to become what he is.

Once man has discovered himself as symbol, he begins to see the world around him as a world of symbols, and so it becomes a meaningful world. For meaning, let us not forget this basic fact, is a dialogical concept. It is originally taken from a context of dialogue in which someone conveys to another what he has in mind. The message conveyed from mind to mind is embodied in a word, a sign, a symbol. The one who sends the message and the one who receives it must agree on the use of the sign by some sort of convention. It is in the sign that the meeting of minds takes place.

If we call anything meaningful we are necessarily setting it into the context of sign, message, and convention. Leave out one of these constituents, and you will see that we can no longer speak of meaning. This is true even in the border case of, let us say, a check mark in your calendar, by which you are reminding yourself of an appointment. The check mark is the sign; the appointment is the message; but unless you establish some sort of convention with yourself, the sign will be meaningless to you when you see it again.

What, then, could be the "convention" (if indeed one exists) by which the world as symbol shall become meaningful to me? We have the symbol and we ask for a message, but what could possibly constitute the foregone agreement (and between whom and whom) as to the meaning of the world as symbol? We must be aware of the weight of this question. Here lies the crucial point of a crisis in which not only meaning and absurdity of the world for me is in the balance but the question of ultimate meaning or absurdity of my own existence. And this is precisely the point where worship comes into focus. For if there is an inner agreement on the basis of which the world as sign will yield its meaning, it can only lie in the oneness of the Mystery-beyond with the Mystery-within; it can only lie in the hidden communication between the Mystery on which all reality is floating, and the Mystery I am to myself in my own innermost depth. To push through to this oneness of Mystery means the discovery of a "con-vention" profound enough and all-embracing enough to guarantee the meaningfulness of everything and of every event. And this "pushing through" is worship.

What else has been the universal function of worship throughout the ages, the one constant, independent of its bewildering changes of form? We are on solid ground if we affirm: the traditional function of worship has been to give meaning to man's life through encounter with Mystery, and this encounter takes place through symbol and symbolic action. By putting it in this way we are focusing as clearly as possible on the central issue, while leaving the boundaries of what might be included in our concept of worship as flexible as we can. Potentially anything whatsoever can become symbol in the context of worship and mediate meaning. All that is needed is an inner gesture on the part of worshiping man, by which he opens himself, makes himself receptive for meaning, assumes the attitude we touched upon when speaking of leisure and of celebration.

Once this is stated it sounds almost too simple to be true.

But you can apply a simple test. Take any experience of your past that qualifies as "worship," and see if it fits. These conditions will have to be fulfilled: your worship experience will have to exhibit the characteristics we claimed for worship; it will have to be an encounter with Mystery that gives meaning to life, and it will have to be mediated through symbol (how could it be otherwise?), through some thing or event which "embodies" this meaning in an ineffable way. If, moreover, you find yourself prepared to call any experience which exhibits these characteristics "worship," we have proved our point.

I for my part would like to introduce as an example the experience of a Japanese Tea Ceremony. It recommends itself because of its points of comparison with the service at the coffeehouse, but above all because it is not stamped as "worship" beforehand. A brief description will suffice. The setting is also that of an academic community, in this case Columbia University. The place, the Faculty-Student Lounge of the Institute for Asian Studies. The time, early afternoon. The attendance, twenty-five to thirty people. The tea master, Mr. Hisashi Yamada of Kyoto. . . . The hum of conversation in the audience dies down quite a while before the tea master ascends the raised platform on which the ceremony is to take place. Two students, already familiar with the Tea Ceremony, represent the guests. The tea master carries in the tray with utensils. He bows to the guests. Kneeling in front of the brazier on which the water is boiling, he prepares a large cup of tea for each of the guests—powdered tea, whisked with a bamboo brush. He offers to each guest a wafer and the cup. Then he washes the bowls, cleans the utensils, bows, and carries the tray out again.

This is all. Hardly a word is spoken. Hardly a word of explanation is needed. The gestures are sparse, determined by an extreme economy of movement. The audience is not "actively involved." Yet, something profound seems to have happened. What was it? A Benedictine monk, trying to describe what happened in the Japanese Tea Ceremony, I find myself paradoxically quoting our young Unitarian friend who tried to describe Vespers at a Benedictine monastery: The spell of the ceremony seemed irresistible "not simply because its forms were beautiful, but because they seemed at once mysterious and full of meaning."

What gave you the sudden assurance that you had never before heard water speaking to water like the water that flowed from the bamboo dipper back into the bronze kettle? Maybe it was simply the highly disciplined leisure in which this gesture took place. And what made you listen to this soliloquy of the water like one long initiated into its language with all the innuendoes of its subtle shades of meaning? Whatever it was, you got the message. And it was not a message that could be translated into any other terms. To say that it had a meaning might mislead one. It comes closer to the truth to say that it had every meaning. It was meaning-full. Am I merely talking about an experience of heightened awareness? Heightened awareness indeed, but more than that: profound gratitude. Maybe this gratitude is the surest touchstone for any genuine encounter with the mystery of life. No wonder the one gesture most frequently recurring during the Tea Ceremony is a basic gesture of worship, the deep bow of grateful awareness.

Admittedly, these are merely subjective remarks. But where we are concerned with the impact of personal experience, this seems the best we can do. It will explain, at any rate, why I do not hesitate to recognize in the Tea Ceremony an experience of worship, even though the more specific notes of worship within my own cultural heritage are not applicable to it. Admittedly, it would make my task easier if I could call the service at the coffeehouse "worship" with equal assurance.

But I can't. Presupposing a detailed description of the event elsewhere in these pages, I will merely add personal notes from which it should become clear why for me it did not become worship in the sense of an encounter with Mystery giving meaning to life.

Maybe the decisive point is that the encounter with Mystery can take place only in and through symbol, as we have seen. At the coffeehouse service, however, the leisure was lacking in which any of the countless symbols and symbolic actions potentially present in that situation were able to come to themselves and to reveal their meaning. It was a go-go affair from the very start, and this seemed to be part of the plan. There was to be "action"—that was evident. Something was to happen. Maybe I resented the fact that so much happened at once that no one thing had time to unfold.

But I must be just. There were a few symbolic moments that stood up with a quiet strength. As we were waiting for the service to begin, some of the young people started to pass flowers around. There was a timeless depth to this gesture. Or the reading from the Book of Job in Hebrew: to hear the word of Scripture in its original sound meant a surprising confrontation. It made you literally sit up. For me the most amazing part of the service, and also the most enjoyable one, was the humming of the congregation during the reading of the Epistle. It proved truly a response, yet more than a response. It was at the same time support of the Reader, approval, hum of agreement, hum of a great swarm of bees; the self-forgetfulness of bees lost in golden pollen was in this hum, and the warmth of the dark hive, the strength of being many. . . . And all this does not even come close to conveying the best of it, which cannot be translated into anything other than a hum.

One symbol used by the Mime Troupe stands out: In "A Son Says Goodbye to His Mother," the soldier approaches a village. A voice announces: "This is the village"; the crank turns and the picture shows—a woman. There was a sudden hush. But the show went on relentlessly. The round too, at the end, was a truly symbolic experience. It created its own silence around itself, and in it there was space to listen. However, as I am enumerating these meaningful moments (and I am doing so with gratitude), it becomes evident that they are not integral parts of one another or of the whole. What held things together was something external, an Order of Service, unrelated, so it seemed to me, to the setting, to the people present, to the situation. Admittedly, the traditional forms of Christian worship are highly complex. Maybe this is where the challenge lies: to strip it to the bare essentials, and to celebrate those—word, bread and wine—with the power and purity with which the tea master celebrated the cup of tea.

It seems remarkable to me in retrospect that none of the supposed highpoints of the service made any impression on me. The reading of the Gospel was lost. With all the noise before and after in that room it would have had to be proclaimed through several loudspeakers at once to stand out; but why not rather tone down the general level of noise? The Consecration—there was nothing to give it prominence, not even, it would seem, special attention on the part of the Celebrant. No one can blame him, considering all the distractions, but I do remember watching him grab bread and wine in a careless way and thinking: What a contrast to the firm and disciplined grip with which the deacon held the ladder while fixing some lights before the service started. Communion was awkward, clumsy, and disorganized. It takes a great deal of preparation to be spontaneous.

I remember leaving the coffeehouse and standing in one of those avenues of bare trees that make Ann Arbor so beautiful in late autumn. It was not at all as if I had just come

out of a worship service, but as if, after hours of noise, I
had suddenly stepped into the nave of an ancient cathedral,
high, silent. I looked around. There was everything needed
for worship: space, silence—and leisure enough to let worship
unfold. If we but let it, worship worships. Who needs you and
me?

# THE LORD'S SONG
# IN A STRANGE LAND

## by Harvey H. Guthrie, Jr.

*Harvey Guthrie, well-known Old Testament scholar and Dean of Episcopal Theological School in Cambridge, took sharp exception to the emphasis Bellah and Brother David placed on the experience of holiness and mystery, insisting, "We cannot discuss worship or engage in worship without inquiring about the myth we are espousing, without evaluating what it implies." In the biblical myth, he said, ". . . the world, the saeculum, within which man exists is invested with the significance elsewhere attributed to a supramundane world." Perhaps, he suggested, today's political demonstrations are the most appropriate models for worship within this myth.*—ED.

### I

RELIGION CANNOT be discussed without reference to the culture within which it exists. Worship cannot, therefore, be discussed without reference to the culture within which it takes place. We must begin there.

To put it in its broadest terms, our culture—"Western culture"—is in exile from its value systems. The figure of exile, the most fitting figure for characterizing our cultural situation, comes of course out of the experience of Judaism. It does not denote merely physical removal from one's homeland, but temporal and spiritual separation from a situation in which the empirical order in which a people lives is the bearer of life's ultimate meaning. Israel lived in such an order until the fall of Jerusalem in 587/6 B.C. To "do theology," ancient Israel recounted her history, updating the story in the successive eras of her existence. Central to her worship was "thanksgiving" (*todah*), the recital of the acts of her God, acts which were not sacral in some dichotomous sense but explanatory precisely of what she was now, empirically, socially, politically. When Jerusalem fell, that order was broken in such a way that empirical, social, political reality was no longer coterminous with being Israel. A people was in exile from the order that had created it. That order became a thing removed from where the people found themselves, something preserved self-consciously in a canon of writings. Religion, for which there was no word when the constitutive order prevailed, became a self-consciously protected reality. Worship in the earlier sense was no longer possible, the Temple becoming something remembered in meetings in the synagogue.

There is neither space nor necessity here to identify the point at which the "modern" world began, but it is true that Western man entered into an analogous situation when factors as different as nominalism in philosophy, the rise of separate nations, the Reformation, the Enlightenment, critical historical method, modern science, technology, and then cybernetics produced a culture related to but different from the one in which Western civilization had gained its distinctive identity. In the new culture Western man found himself in exile from the situation in which his value systems—theoretical as well as practical, philosophical as well as religious and ethical—had been formulated. Because the new culture was secular, this was especially true of the religious heritage of the West. Western man as religious man found himself in exile from the order that had formed him and, beginning at the Reformation and Counter-Reformation, he sought to maintain the integrity of that order within which he was no longer empirically living. In classic Protestantism the canon of sacred writings came self-consciously to be regarded as the place where the constitutive Christian reality, now not there in empirical existence, was to be apprehended. In Roman Catholicism something analogous happened both in the self-conscious definition of teaching authority in the church and in the codification of the church's liturgical life in one, authorized missal. In Anglicanism the Book of Common Prayer came *de facto* to serve a similar purpose.

In all these developments a people, separated by the movement of history from the order productive of their identity, sought to maintain that identity. In a very real sense the situation was one of exile, one in which worship was not the celebration of the present order as the means through which God was related to the world but the remembrance of how God *had* done that through a past order. The situation was one of exile in which "church" was a gathering of the people of God who did not know, though they were tolerated and even honored in the new culture, how really to sing the Lord's songs in a strange land. Both the developments in Roman Catholicism focused in the First Vatican Council and the rise of dialectical theology in Protestantism represent vigorous responses to the new situation at the point at which its existence became unavoidably apparent. Fundamentalism and "spiky" ritualism represent more "gut" responses to the situation.

Another way to make the point is to say that modern culture is not, to use Tillich's term, theonomous. That culture is a unique thing on the human scene, even though it has now become through Western expansion pretty much the culture of the whole planet. It is unique in that those who live in it are practical, if not theoretical, atheists. They do not view life in their empirical dealings with it—politically, scientifically, technologically—as if there were a God. That is as true of theoretical theists as it is of theoretical atheists. We are all *practical* atheists, when we turn on the weather forecast, when we drive our cars, when we turn to the psychiatrist, when fuses blow even in church buildings. That is what most profoundly makes modern culture a *secular* culture. And that is why Western man, not just religious Western man, is in exile. His value systems were formed in a culture that was not secular, that was theistic, and he finds himself in exile from those value systems. It is to that situation that C. P. Snow, for example, addresses himself when he speaks of "two cultures," the culture of the humanists and the culture of the scientists. In classic academia as well as in church, Western man is remembering rather than participating in the order from which he takes his identity, or from which he *has* taken his identity. He is a practical atheist, and his culture is secular.

Worship, in terms of most of the definitions to which we are accustomed, is not indigenous to atheism or secularism. That is why worship as we know it—for the most part in forms inherited from a more or less theonomous culture—is so fake to the children of our age. That is also why so many of those who engage in worship in our culture cling to the inherited forms so defensively. That is why there is probably a high correlation in our culture between worshipers and reactionaries, why a Hitler or a Wallace can find so many backers among churchgoers. Both those who are explicit about their atheism and secularism and those who react to modern culture may be clearer about the issues than liberal synthesizers.

## II

But there may be something to be said that is neither nihilistic nor reactionary, and, at the same time, not naïvely synthetic. Various trends in contemporary theological thinking perceive, if ever so dimly, a *quartum quid* which could have tremendous consequences for the meaning of worship in an atheistic, secular culture. It can be argued that modern culture is atheistic and secular precisely as a result of the fact that its religious heritage is biblical, prophetic, Judaeo-Christian. To put it dramatically, the religious heritage of Western culture is, in its fundamentals, not "religious" in the usual sense of the word. It is to that conclusion that the results of more than a century of critical work on the Bible in the light of its cultural context point, and it is in that direction that essays in constructive theology by those as different as the Lutheran Dietrich Bonhoeffer and the Jesuit Johannes Metz point.

Myth can be defined in the widest sense as the explanation given by a people for the way things are, the story accounting for the tragedies a people faces in this world and for the things a people celebrates in worship. Almost invariably, whether in the ancient Near East or in classical Greece, the myths associated with religions and cults take the world in which man lives to be the result of and something continually reflected by what transpires in another world outside it, above it. The real action, the action that forms things and accounts for things, takes place in the world of the gods (*theoi*). It is the doings, the decisions, the struggles of the gods that result in the cycle of nature, which is the setting of human life. The myth recites those doings, and the cult represents and celebrates them. The function of worship and of spirituality is to put man in touch with that other world, which is "real" and which is ultimately significant. And that continues to be the function of worship and spirituality when human rationality demythologizes the myth, when its implications are conceptualized abstractly. What the *theoi* are all about and what their doings are all about is centered in the concept of God (*theos*). *The*ism in the cultural heritage of Western man arises out of such a myth.

The biblical myth, however, is about *a* Someone so unique and so particular that using the category *theos* to talk about him only results in confusion. The prophets kept insisting on that as ancient Israel became a part of Near Eastern culture and inevitably began to use the *theo*logical categories of that culture to talk about that Someone, Yahweh. The earliest generations of the Christian movement insisted on that as the employment of the *theo*logical categories of the Hellenistic world to talk about the significance of Jesus Christ threatened to obscure the central affirmation that that particular Someone had definitively related himself to the world in a specific and particular and empirical series of events beginning with Jesus and continuing in the Church.

The biblical myth recounts, when it does use the *theo*logical concepts of the culture in which it exists, how that Someone has done away with the gods, the *theoi* (cf. Psalm 82). The biblical myth proclaims that that Someone has assigned to men and to the human enterprise the role and significance reserved for the gods in other myths—that is the real significance of what is specifically being said in Genesis 1:26 and what is implicitly there all through the Bible. In the biblical myth, significance is taken away from that world of which other myths speak. Precisely the world, the *saeculum,* within which man exists is invested with the significance elsewhere attributed to a supramundane realm. In the biblical myth, the heavenly realm is divested of its importance; and nature, which in the other myths is taken to be the result and reflection of that realm, is desacralized. Human decisions and actions are given sacral significance. Secularism, the location of significance in this *saeculum,* has in fact, and probably only could have, arisen on a cultural soil whose religious heritage was biblical.

The results of recent historical investigation show that the basic biblical category for the relation between man and the

Someone of whom the Bible speaks—the covenant—is a *po-litical* category. The covenant formularies of the Old Testament, such as the classic one in the Ten Commandments, are exactly parallel to treaties between political overlords and subject kingdoms. Thus, the medium being a significant part of the message, Israel was insisting that the relationship obtaining between herself and Yahweh (the proper, specific name of that Someone) was not the kind of relationship expressed in the cosmic myths. It was not a relationship in which the gods were present in the forces and cycles of nature over which man had no real control. It was a relationship in which human decisions and actions, and a demand to which they were responses, were the stuff of theology. It was not, in the usual sense of the word, a religious relationship. It was a relationship analogous to the relationships in the political realm. Yahweh was more like an emperor than a god of the usual type: thus the great troubles attendant upon insistence that Jews or Christians acknowledge another emperor as divine. It was a relationship in which the secular was invested with significance.

Worship in the biblical tradition is not, therefore, a means of celebrating or making contact with a realm above this world in which real significance is located. Worship in the biblical tradition is a situation in which a human community is addressed with a demand that imparts significance to that community's response, whether the response be positive or negative. It is an occasion for both penitence and thanksgiving, a divine accusation of men's disobedience taking place precisely because a divine imperative has redeemed what man does from meaninglessness. Worship in the biblical tradition is a situation in which a human community is given a hope by being placed proleptically into the time at which its Hero will have won in *this* game, the time in light of which all the times leading to it are rendered significant. The elation in that worship—whether at the old Israel's covenant festival or the new Israel's Supper of the Lord—is the elation of a crowd hearing the candidate on the platform not only as a candidate but as the next president. It is an elation which, precisely because it celebrates a victory present but not yet present, has in it a demand for dedication and action between the present and the election that is coming. To put it negatively, the elation in biblical worship is not an elation at having somehow denied or forgotten or transcended the conditions of humanness. It is not an apolitical elation. From Amos' censure of indulgence in orgiastic fertility rites to Paul's insistence that five intelligible words are of more value than thousands of words spoken in the language of ecstasy, the biblical tradition refuses to recognize as authentic worship any escapist technique by which the significance of human rationality and responsibility is implicitly denied.

### III

Modern men are practical atheists, secularists, and they are such precisely because of the impact of the biblical myth upon the culture that has formed them. Worship of the kind arising from the more usual religious myth, the myth that locates significance in the world of the gods, is something strange to modern man. Yet modern man can, in his situation of exile, yearn for a significance he himself cannot manufacture to be given to his life. In that yearning he can be very naïve about what is so foreign to him.

It is easy for those to whom it comes so unnaturally to think of *all* worship as one thing, and to be simplistically for it or against it. But there are worships and worships, just as there have been gods and gods. Worship always implies a myth in the sense in which the word has been used above. Myths differ significantly, and the biblical myth is uniquely different in imparting significance to this *saeculum*. It is a terrible as well as a wonderful thing, as the Gospel parable points out, to live in a house swept clean of demons. The terror involved, the situation of exile, can result in confusion between myths and myths and between worships and worships. Let us be as blunt as Amos or Paul. The Dionysiac myth, whether in its ancient form or in more modern forms, is not the biblical myth. The Gnostic myth, whether in ancient or modern dress, is not the biblical myth. We cannot discuss worship or engage in worship without inquiring about the myth we are espousing, without evaluating what it implies. The biblical myth does not indicate a route by which man can escape the conditions of humanness and the ambiguities of the human enterprise. It announces that the One who ultimately matters has come right into the conditions of humanness, has invaded the human enterprise and so invested it with meaning. Worship, therefore—or spirituality, which provides by whatever means a "trip" away from humanness— is a route that leads away from what exiled man is really seeking. The theologian at Uppsala who refused to equate fondling Swedish girls with the worship of Almighty God had a very real point, and the relevance of that point to worship has nothing to do with the evil of an unbiblical puritanism that denies the beauty of Swedish girls or the glow produced by a martini or the ecstasy of the boogaloo. The point is that worship involves a choice between myths. The Someone of whom the biblical myth speaks is not Apollo, and it is fashionable today to point that out. But that does not mean that he is Dionysus.

## IV

All that is by way of a caveat, albeit a very necessary caveat. The real point is that an exploration of the biblical myth and its implications can lead to the conclusion that modern man is not really in exile at all, at least not in the way he is prone to think. His practical atheism and his secularity, if he faces them and does not run from them, if he seeks their origins and refuses to drift, may exist because of a Someone who slays the gods and glorifies this *saeculum*. It may be that he is uncomfortable in church just because Someone has desacralized what man mistakenly thinks *ought* to be sacral, just because that Someone is there in what modern man in his secularity *really* believes is significant.

It is the discovery that what had appeared for so long to be exile is not really exile at all that is beginning to revolutionize worship in the 1960's. If our situation is not really one of exile, then the books and institutions and set rites within which we sought (rightly) to preserve the integrity of that from which we were separated lose their usefulness. Simply redoing the interior of a sanctuary will not revitalize worship if the very concept of a sanctuary misses the point of where the One worshiped is present. Simply updating the language of a Prayer Book will not revitalize worship if the conditions that produced Prayer Books no longer really obtain. If we are not really in a strange land, then the Lord's songs may be sung where we are, not just read from a book that preserves how they *were* sung in a homeland from which we are separated. We are at a stage of the game that is both promising and painful. We are beginning to discover that to be pilgrims is not the same as being exiles. We have discovered that through finding what is at the heart of a tradition, but we are discovering also that we will lose that if we merely seek to preserve the tradition.

We are at a point at which we can see that what is very modern and secular and nonreligious is not incompatible with the tradition. We are at a point at which the San Francisco Mime Troupe can show us that the involvement of all of us in what is focused in Vietnam has something to do with praying, "Almighty God . . . from whom no secrets are hid," at

which sacrificial protest against what the protesters believe
to be present injustice may be directly related to "for in the
night in which he was betrayed . . . ." We are at a point at
which it is becoming possible to appreciate that uncomforta-
bleness experienced by the Israel of old when Someone insisted that the real stuff of this *saeculum* was the source of
accountability that made being human significant.

We are at a point at which worship will increasingly not
have the comforting aura of exilic predictability, precisely
because we are finding that the One we worship is present
with his demand in this changing *saeculum*. We must not re-
treat from such a time into "religion," for in so doing we will
be retreating from that One. We are in a time in which, both
for those who are comfortable with them and for those who
object to them, the inherited forms—however theoretically
sound—will look "religious" in a nonbiblical way. Precisely
as an adherent of the biblical myth, I have to recognize that
we are in a time in which many are not going to be able to
worship at all with integrity, even if they worry about that
more than in previous times. The One I have been talking
about is not going to be able to make his point in our culture
unless we are willing to give him room to do it. Where such
willingness will lead, it is impossible to say. But it is clear
that the biblical myth insists that religion and politics must
be mixed, that this *saeculum* is significant, that no worship is
better than worship constructed on some other premise than
that, that the will of the One who is God has to do with
mercy and not sacrifice.

# WORSHIP AS CELEBRATION AND CONFRONTATION

## by Howard Moody

*Howard Moody, Minister of the Judson Memorial Church in Greenwich Village and a recognized leader in liturgical innovation, gave a more muscular interpretation to Guthrie's position. He insisted that we must have a "desacralized worship" marked by celebration and confrontation. He felt that the setting and music of the coffeehouse service facilitated celebration and that the presentations of the Mime Troupe confronted us effectively with ourselves and our world.—ED.*

No ASPECT of the Church's life so tellingly reveals its major problem as does its worship. It is here that the schizophrenia of the Church becomes evident and one glimpses the real dichotomy between the Church's liturgy and its life, the way in which we have kept worship pure and unsullied from the shock and trauma of contemporary life. While the world reels under the blows of cataclysm and change, the Church keeps her worship quiet and eternally the same. If the contemporary theological ferment and the social revolution are taken seriously, we must expect that the current understanding of what characterizes the Church will be shaken up, and her life and ways of being in the world radically altered. It is my conviction that the worship of Holy One of Israel will remain a vital part of the life of the Christian community, but it will be a *desacralized* worship. Worship and worldliness will be wedded in an inextricable manner. In such a ritual we shall acknowledge the power of that Reality who for us is the source of our creation, our redemption, and whatever hope we have; we shall celebrate a mystery called Grace that keeps interrupting the tragedy and despair of our lives with epiphanies of joy and meaning. The concomitant of the statement that our worship is the worship of God is that this worship apart from man, his needs, his hungers, his world, is obscure and irrelevant. We bring to worship our *work* and our *world*. The world belongs to worship and worship belongs to the world.

Some iconoclasts insist we must get rid of all ritual and cultic acts and simply have a "religionless gathering." On the other hand, there are those that insist that the cultic act of worship is a precondition to being a Christian and absolutely prerequisite to being the Church. I think neither of these alternatives is acceptable. As for the abolition of ritual, as long as man is the symbolic animal that he is, that's not apt to happen; and as for worship (the cultic act) being necessary in order to be the Church (cf. Paul's circumcision debate in Romans) I doubt if any activity we might devise or organize could guarantee the reality of the Church and I am certain that Bonhoeffer was biblically grounded when he drew from Paul's inferences that to be a Christian is not to be religious or cultic in a certain way.

But I believe we will see a certain desacralizing of worship taking place. Harvey Cox in *Worship in a Secular Age* is pointing in the right direction when he claims that worship as a cultic act must be relativized, i.e., shorn of its sacral, religious character so that it is recognized as a fully human activity (as part of the world and not divine in any sense). That is also the Old Testament understanding of worship. When religious people, whether clergy or clericalized laity, insist upon the cultic act of worship as being "divine" and essentially different from the other human acts in which God is honored and served, they distort the meaning. The "secularizing" of cultic acts is very common in the biblical narrative. Dr. Walter Horrelson points out how the Sabbath was desacralized: "Rest and refreshment God bestows on his people. He sanctifies the seventh day not for religion but for man and beast in their daily life. The holiness of the seventh day consists precisely in its being a free day, free for living, resting . . . it was actually a socio-ethical day not a religious one."

The biblical understanding of worship will also keep us from dogmatizing or absolutizing "worship" as a cultic act. That criterion is to be found in Romans 12, namely, "With eyes wide open to the mercies of God, I beg you, my brothers, as an act of intelligent worship, to give him your bodies as a living sacrifice consecrated to and acceptable to him." Here is true worship, that to which the cultic act should point. It might be better to call the action when we gather *communication* or *celebration,* rather than worship. What is important is that we appreciate the fact that none of the prescribed worship forms (in various Christian traditions) is a permanent mark of the Church. The true test of an act of worship is whether or not it prepares us for presenting our bodies as a living sacrifice in the service of God's world. We will be able to rediscover this true meaning only as we can liberate worship from sacral impediments that have turned it into a religious performance.

There are several fundamental factors that have influenced the changing styles of worship in the contemporary church. First, intellectually, the theological agitation of the recent period and radical theology have brought under question the very mode and manner of our worship.

Second, here in America the social revolution marked by the civil rights movement had some effects. Clergy and laity who were immersed in the movement in the early 1960's were exposed to new kinds of worship experiences. I remember one night in May, 1963, standing in the 16th Street Baptist Church in Birmingham, Alabama, after a day of demonstrating and the mass arrest of eight hundred children. It was called a "civil rights rally" but it was a strange mixture of prayer meeting, clambake, and political pep rally in which the power and meaning of true worship broke through all the unorthodox and unacceptable forms of that dramatic three-hour meeting. The rock-'n'-roll spirituals were secularized hymns; the loud, emotive prayers were political petitions, the speeches and testimonies were morale builders preparing the troops for action against the "powers and principalities of darkness." The altar call was an invitation for people to go to jail or "to present your bodies as a living sacrifice which is your true worship." It was a profound experience, and the next Sunday morning at Judson Church, New York City, the excitement, the power, the emotional impact of complete joyousness in the face of danger were missing. Our service, though billed as the worship of God seemed insipid, dull, and unrelated by comparison. Only when worship is molded and shaped by the happenings of the world is it likely to be meaningful.

Third, the Church's increasing engagement in recent times with the arts (music, painting, drama, poetry) has dynamically influenced Christian liturgy. At Judson Church we owe a great deal in our experimentation in worship to the sensitive craftsmen who worked in our theaters and gallery. Samuel Miller said that faith without art is dumb, that is, uncommunicative. Without the arts the Church has no language adequate for the communication of her essential realities. It was the artists at Judson who first probed the purpose of our worship and its relations to the rest of our life together. These people, in searing honesty, demanded that symbols mean something, that language say something, that liturgy be alive. The point of their questions became clear when it was obvious that their dance creations and dramas were more unashamedly joyful in the praise of Creation than a hundred well-ordered and theologically correct worship services, and we became concerned that the arts themselves in all their power might help to redeem our worship and awaken us to radically new ways of seeing reality.

These three influences then—the theological ferment of the 1950's, the social revolution (especially the freedom movement), and the influence of the arts—have been the significant factors in worship experimentation and liturgical radicalism.

Let us turn now to what I believe is happening to worship as an activity when this experimental openness is present. I want to discuss what forms "desacralization" is taking and examine the evidence of it in the Canterbury service.

1. *Space.* One serious drawback to liturgical renewal is the sanctuary. One way of sacralizing and divinizing worship (making it untouchable and thus unreformable) is to put it in a spatial context that is considered peculiarly sanctified. There is something about the juxtaposition of stained-glass windows, altar, and pews combined with "hushed lighting" which turns ordinary square footage into sacrosanct space to be used only or primarily for the exalted activity of "divine worship"—a room so religious and so reserved that its very atmosphere shapes and defines the nature of the activity that can happen there. In our own church the place where we worship is not a "sanctuary" in the traditional Protestant, churchy sense, nor a place set aside and sanctified for religious rites and acts, but a place made holy by human happenings of every kind. It is a *meeting room* in the fullest and most extensive sense of that word. It is a place where political rallies occur, where community tension explodes, where we memorialize a national tragedy; a place where we eat and

drink and dance and see drama. It is a place where the human sounds of laughter and crying, of praising and cursing, of applause and silence, split the air with regularity.

So many things have happened there that we care about, that have moved our lives, that have changed our minds, that have filled us with meaning—that is why the space is made holy and fitting for our worship. The space at Canterbury House where we worshiped was such space the night before we gathered there to watch the San Francisco Mime Troupe perform a bawdy, political satire on issues tearing our nation apart. The next morning we gathered in the same *space* (still without chairs or pews), undecorated and untransformed by cultic appurtenances, to enact another drama of communion. One could sense that the space there was determined by what happened in it and not vice versa. It is a long and painful process, the freeing of space by the Church so that it might be available to all the world for all kinds of human events, and not a prideful possession preserved for our own sanctities.

2. *Language.* This is one aspect of liturgics that is most difficult to deal with, particularly in the communions where the order of worship is fixed. The Protestant tradition being highly rational and verbal has controlled the Church with words. The problem of semantics has been at the heart of the theological ferment in the past decade and we are seeing a de-jargonization of theology that is bound to affect the liturgy. The Christian's vocabulary is being taken away from him so that "saints at least may think in algebra without sin." The archaic and stilted language of much worship serves only to isolate and alienate people from the basic experience for which Christians gather. This is true not only of the Anglican Prayer Book forms but also of the extemporaneous preaching of the free-church tradition. In the worship experience at Canterbury House, there was a very telling and dramatic incident during the reading of the Prayer of Intercession. In

this prayer there is one of those unconsciously arrogant petitions which requests God to "grant to all Christians to live
in unity, love and concord." And when those words were re-
cited one could feel a quiet wave of repulsion go through the
congregation gathered from many faiths and no faith. What
is more important, the leader of the worship felt it too and in
a most relevant interruption confessed the chauvinism of that
prayer and made it clear we desired that *all people*, not just
Christians, live in love and unity. Not only does too much of
our Christian vocabulary fail to communicate, it also communicates the wrong thing to the listener.

However, there is a further problem with language in liturgy that we must be conscious of. When communication
displaces communion, and words are cheapened by abuse and
misuse, there comes to be a distrust of verbiage. Here the
visual artist, sensitive to the nonverbal, is especially competent
to help us to find effective images. Those who would experiment with worship must be sensitive to the bankruptcy of
words and the power available to us in nonverbal forms.

A most effective utilization of mixed media occurred in the
Canterbury service. During the offering, a color film sliced a
happening from life and exposed our eyes to the experience
while music from the folk-rock group brought sound and sight
together. Visual symbols and acts may redeem our word-
drenched worship and make it more meaningful.

3. *Music.* The cultic ceremonies and rituals of Jews and
Christians have always been filled with music. It is a media
universal in its appeal, evoking emotional depths untouched
by other appeals. In contemporary Protestant worship, music,
like words, is an enigma. Anyone who has attempted to make
reforms and changes in liturgy will come up against music as
the most traditional and inflexible aspect of experimentation.
Just as seminaries staff our churches, so schools of sacred music
staff our choirs and determine the music of our services. I've

been on many a campus in this country to speak at chapel services. In recent years when experimental liturgy has been so widespread, I find that college chapel services are still unchanged, in a place where tradition is less troublesome and youth is open. In my inquiries I always hear the chaplain saying, "Well, I would like to experiment but the head of the music department directs the choir and he won't hear of it." Those who believe that the only appropriate music for worship in the twentieth century is sixteenth- and eighteenth-century choral anthems and hymns written by Bach or Beethoven are anachronistic. Sounds change like the usage of words and new sounds grow out of new life. The so-called sacred music no longer calls forth in modern man the images of reality that it once did. Music is made sacred by its associations with life and human events that fill it with meaning. "A Mighty Fortress" may be a noble comment on the Reformation struggle, but "We Shall Overcome" is a more appropriate hymn and one closer to the people of the 1960's. We ought to be free enough to appropriate all kinds of music to overcome the false dichotomies between religion and life, between the sacred and the secular. We have to set our creative musical talent loose in the Church to write new music to the glory of God and all his creation, unencumbered by limitations of religious music. The new hymn "When the Changes Come" by Al Carmines, a very talented composer-musician at Judson, which was commissioned by the Presbyterian Church, is illustrative of the new type of hymnody that churches could elicit from artists if they are freed from hang-ups with sacred music. The hymns sung at the Canterbury service did have the new sound of today's youth.

Not only must we be liberated in the range of our music, but also in the instruments we use. In most churches the organ is deemed the only "appropriate" instrument for worship. Are not all instruments suitable for the praise of God? Why only the organ, which is so imitative of other instruments? The church organ is a beautiful instrument, but it does not exhaust the musical possibilities open to us, and with certain music it is a dismal failure. Guitars, recorders, harps, drums, brass are all potentially rich contributors to services with music.

The desacralizing process taking place in cultic experiments today is not important in itself, but only insofar as it helps us to recover the essential qualities of an authentic worship experience; and the two qualities that I think have been suppressed in most worship today are the sense of celebration and of confrontation.

Our worship is nonparticipatory performance ordered and planned to perfection, guaranteed not to challenge or embarrass or involve the observer beyond the narrow limits of his rational comprehension (with only a few strains on that!). Christian worship is full of symbols that have been tamed and domesticated so as not to disturb our feelings or our life style. The images we employ have been trivialized and there is present no symbol of Reality that captures our minds and captivates our spirits so that our bodies move with a new purpose in this world. Worship has been and could be again such a ritual of power and meaning for life. Our spirits are hungry enough, our emotions are starved enough, our bodies are feeling enough, that we long for the cleansing of a true Ritual, if only we could break through. The late Samuel Miller expressed this hope for worship in his poetic style:

If worship could be brought alive . . . if the dead smothering blubber of respectability could be sloughed off it, if it could once again stand the naked soul before God; if the rushing torrents of man's sins and doubts could pour through his broken prayers, if a new honesty like a strong antiseptic could bathe away the suppurating sores of pious vanity and ecclesiastical foppery—in such worship, human at every level, the image they have adored might come to life again and clutch their souls with eternal mercy.*

* *The Dilemma of Modern Belief* (New York: Harpers, 1963), p. 36.

This is the lively hope of every person who worships in the expectancy that his vision and his hearing and his feeling will be enhanced and sensitized by the experience.

We will go a long way toward realization of our hopes for worship reform if we can recover the sense of celebration that characterized it originally in the Old Testament. One could stereotype our church services today, but we would be near the truth about them if we characterized them as being pious, mournful, sterile, and joyless. All of us know exceptions, but most of our experience testifies to the dullness and deadness of church ritual.

The closest resemblance to the Old Testament feel for celebration in ceremony in recent times is the Hasidic sect of modern Judaism and the unadulterated (by whites) Negro services. Both rituals exemplify an overflowing joy about life which for the most part is hard, difficult, and ghettoized. Ralph Moore, speaking about the nature of worship, suggests that it is a "kind of celebrative kick, a jovial good natured profoundly hilarious laughter in the presence of murky devils." He goes on in his reflections about worship to say:

There is after all a merriment which is possible for living life even when one aspect of life is excruciating pain. Our traditional words —praise, thanksgiving, eucharist—are older words which mean these things for the contemporary situation. To think of the wandering desert bands, subjected to all manner of hellish trials, taking a respite to breathe, reflect, clap hands, and sing in joyous defiance of the forces that would destroy them is to recover the primal motivation for worship, a spontaneity of movement rarely seen in institutionalized religion but recognized again today in all kinds of public gatherings, both sacred and profane.*

But for white Christians reared in a worship tradition of solemnity and quietness, any noises or sounds that split the silence or mar the mood so assiduously created and manipulated are as out of place as obscenities in a Sunday school

* *Worship as a Celebrative Kick* (unpublished mimeo-monograph).

lesson. We need to recover some images in our past. Take
the worship described in Revelation 4 and 5. Now there was
celebration, a really noisy and joyful, swinging activity. All
those creatures, and angels and archangels, and elders cut
loose with everything they had and the heavens jumped with
their hosannas. It makes an "acid high" look like a Methodist
vesper service; and it is mixed-media with a vengeance! It's
very interesting that, when we talk about traditional worship,
these kinds of experiences recorded in the New Testament
and the great festivals and feast days of the Old Testament
are never considered part of "tradition."

In the worship at Canterbury House we recaptured some
of the verve of the Hasidim, some of the emotional release
of the Negro service, and people danced and sang at the close
of the service because that's how it made them feel. At least
part of the freedom to celebrate in ways not usually associated
with worship came from the *space* in which it took place
(open, uncluttered, undeterminative); the language both verbal and nonverbal; and the music with its effervescent, con-
tagious rock-beat and folk quality.

Finally, a word about the ritual of confrontation. Worship
as confrontation, though theologically and biblically correct,
runs against the grain of our present concept of the meaning
of worship. The atmosphere, arrangement, architecture, lighting, and music of our services today remove the worshiper
from the world, its cares, troubles, and tragedy. At worst these
services are pure escapism and at best soothers of the ruffled
psyches of the people. The cultic-act worship, however, ought
to be the place of honest confrontation of *ourselves,* with all
our embarrassments and ambiguities, and *our world* with its
inhumanity and tragedy. We can escape ourselves in words
(especially if they are archaic enough) and cover our "sick
and bent world" (like Linus' security blanket) with prayers
and music. Rituals and ceremonies can lie about us and our

world and what God demands, but an authentic ritual is one where Reality is wrestled with like Jacob by the river Jabbok, struggling for the naked truth about himself and his place in the world. Right in the middle of our swinging, joyous service at Canterbury House, the San Francisco Mime Troupe acted out the trial of the Catonsville Nine. It kept in serious perspective the real world and real worship. Worship as celebration need not exclude confrontation—they belong together. Real worship will hold the two together in painful contradiction and thus the double-edged truth about our lives.

As we experiment and break through the encrusted traditions (recent) that restrict our Christian rituals, we must all be assured that our God, who is not fussy, accepts all offerings we give to him and each other. Let all pilgrims be on the way!

# WORSHIP AS REVOLUTION

## by Sandra Archer

*Sandra Archer, Director of the San Francisco Mime Troupe, conceived and directed the coffeehouse "sermon" on the Catonsville Nine. She took great exception to the Bellah and Brother David concern for the recovery of the sacred and pushed Guthrie's and Moody's political and secular emphasis about as far as it could go. She felt that worship helped people to sublimate their alienation rather than turn it into revolutionary action and that, therefore, the more "beautiful" worship is, the more reactionary it is. In short, "We need to be disturbed, not fulfilled." Her sermon was an effort to do just that.—*Ed.

MY RELIGION is the revolution, the total political, physical, cultural, spiritual revolution that we must make to free the world from exploitation and our souls from alienation; when all men are brothers we will have found God. True acts of worship are acts of revolution.

Organized religion, where it is not corrupt, still thinks the revolution can be accomplished on the spiritual plane alone. Experimental worship borrows, from group psychology, hippy art, even old-time religion, techniques for making us *feel* brotherhood; experience the satisfaction of true communion.

But what right have we to that brotherly feeling and that satisfaction when we are participating daily in acts of injustice?
Profit off our brothers during the week, hold hands with them
on Sunday. The church maintains the system by maintaining
the individuals in the system, absorbing their guilt and com-
pensating their alienation; the search for "revolutionary"—
i.e., more satisfying—forms of worship and communion can
only end in enabling the church to perform its reactionary
role more effectively. We need to be disturbed, not fulfilled.
Until after the revolution, the only valuable experience is one
which leads to a revolutionary action. The religious experience that is complete in itself, that demands only to be experienced, does not make people change their lives. It is immediately isolated from life; placed in a special category of
"beautiful experience," it is consumed. We need forms which
cannot be swallowed, which are open in a revolutionary direction and demand completion by the witnesses themselves.

The problem of isolability, of people's consuming the experience instead of continuing it, is always with us in the
theater, so much so that it often seems as though aesthetic
success guaranteed moral failure: the more beautiful the piece,
the more passive the response. The mime described below,
designed and performed as part of a worship service at Ann
Arbor Canterbury House, attempted to break the double
frame of religious service and theatrical performance by making people take an action.

## MIME
### To be performed in a room filled with people sitting on the floor (no stage)

*Original Concept:* Make Cotton into Cement, or . . . How
     to Reach and Affect a System that Absorbs Everything
     One Does.

Specifically, how to change a cultural pattern in Canterbury House from acceptance of any theatrical activity as entertainment to participation in the revolution.

MIME: Four men in street clothes, wearing white headbands, rise from a squatting position, forming a perfect square with their bodies, facing inward. A drum starts, a lone note separated from the men, muffled, slow, hitting on the fourth beat of each measure. The men begin to walk in place, shifting weight on the drumbeat. They look at one another and set their walks in rhythm. A voice over a loudspeaker reads an article from *Time* magazine about the Catonsville Nine, a group of Catholic clergy and laymen who have been sentenced and fined for pouring homemade napalm on the local draft-board files. Father Berrigan, the Catholic priest who led the Nine, used as his defense this sentence: "Some property has no right to exist." The judge in counseling the jury reminded them that their duty was to the law, and that it was "of no consequence that in the eyes of history these men may be right." During the reading the four men are still walking in place to the hypnotic drumbeat. When the voice finishes, one man moves in the same rhythm over to the man on his left, stands directly in front of him, facing inward, and with his back slowly pushes the second man out of his space. The other men move so as to re-form the square: they adjust for the first man's move. The first man then moves, still in rhythm, across the square and takes a third man's space. The others adjust once again, recreating the square. The first man then moves out of the square and creates a new space. The men form a close triangle and move themselves into a straight line behind the first man. The drum still marks the movements. The first man raises his arms from his sides and opens them, palms up. Slowly he begins to revolve in front of the three; they maintain the solid line behind him. On the fourth turn one hand clenches into a fist and he swings sharply around, hitting all three men with one swing; they fall, splattered, onto the people sitting around them. The first man begins to laugh, an ugly raucous laugh, the drumbeats grow louder but not faster, and the man begins to take heavy steps, his feet stomping on the drumbeat. He steps through the seated bodies to the prone men and takes their white headbands, rips them, and throws the pieces onto the nearest members of the audience. From another part of the room two women in white headbands rise, carrying between them a bucket filled with a white sheet. They move to the wounded men. They tip the bucket and touch the sheet gently to the bodies and faces of the men; the men do not respond. As the women rise from the bodies, the men in unison *"ahh"* a long discordant note lasting three measures. The women move toward the first man, who is stomping his way through the audience. He has by now walked the entire length of the room and when he sees the women his laughter begins again, punctuated by loud inhalations of breath. He moves toward them and pulls the bucket, throwing them off balance. They catch themselves, return to the dead men, pull the bodies into a pile, which they cover with the white sheet. Then they reach their arms out to the man. He turns on them and slaps one so hard that she lets out a scream and falls heavily onto the audience. The other woman pulls her onto the pile and covers all the bodies. The man moves, laughing, stomping around the room, stepping on those who do not move. The woman puts the bucket down beside the bodies and walks toward the man. He expects her submission and turns to receive her. She places her hands on his face; he doesn't look at her but receives this gesture; his arms are now open and out, reaching the corners of the room, filling the room with his power. She slowly pulls his white headband down over his face, moving behind him as she pulls. When the band is around his neck, she twists it violently and chokes him, pulling him down and back. He gags, one hand reaches for the cloth and one grasps the space he has been filling. He falls. The drum stops. The woman looks at him, turns to face the other bodies and, covering her face with her hands, bends slowly down, at once making obeisance to her dead brothers and expressing her grief.

The intention was to rouse the audience to participation, making them either stop the man or move out of his way. There were definite points at which an active response was required from the audience: when the first man knocks down the other three and they fall on the people around them; when he throws the headbands onto the audience; when he moves through the audience stepping on people; when he hits the woman and she falls onto someone. *Question:* If an actor steps on another actor, it's theater, but if an actor steps on an audience member, what is it? *Answer:* It's time for the audience to take an action. I thought people would move aside; I hoped they would stop the man.

The actual performance was a partial failure; the mime depended upon the man's brutality breaking through the fourth wall and touching the audience members; it didn't happen because the actor playing the first man was unable to *step on people.* This failure displayed innate considerateness but it allowed the audience to remain unconcerned with the central theme. At what point do you turn your protest sign around and slam a cop over the head because he is viciously macing and beating the protester next to you?

The constant adjustment of the three men illustrates, at first, the healing power of love, but it is continued past the point where love is fatally inadequate. The final act of the woman strangling the first man shows the action one must take in order to live in a good world. Father Berrigan is an illustration of a man whose actions are commensurate with his beliefs: we must change this society for the good of all men—and we must begin by changing *around us*.

# A WEDDING MASQUE
# FOR LONELY TRAVELERS

## by Nancy Willard Lindbloom

*Nancy Willard Lindbloom, a poet and fictionist who teaches literature and writing at Vassar, was moved by the seminar discussions and coffeehouse service to write a wedding service as her critique. Her wedding masque seems to bring together the Bellah–Brother David concern for symbolic recovery of the holy and the Guthrie–Moody–Archer emphasis on the secular and political in worship. In effect, her masque is a response to Sandy Archer's concern about the corrupting effect of the "beautiful."—*ED.

LAST YEAR I tried to write a wedding service for a friend of mine whose boyfriend was facing a possible prison sentence for resisting the draft. But I am a Quaker and Friends have no liturgy. The bride and groom often write their own vows, which they speak to each other; there is no minister, and much of the service is silent. Not wishing to restrict myself to a liturgy whose structure and uses were unfamiliar to me, I decided to call my service a *masque*. The first time I saw a good production of *The Tempest*, I knew that every couple should have a masque written for them. I owe a great deal to the service at Canterbury House in Ann Arbor, Michigan, put together by the chaplain there and the San Francisco Mime Troupe, for it was only after participating in their service that I had a clear idea of how to write mine.

Well, why a masque? In this case, because the traditional Protestant wedding services did not take into account the special circumstances surrounding this marriage: the groom seemed about to be jailed for a crime of conscience, and that was too important to be left out.

But there is another reason, suggested by the word itself. Since magic has been replaced by science, I think the quickest way to transform yourself or anyone else into another shape—that gift of Proteus lost when people no longer believed in magic—is to put on a mask. When I lived in Santa Fe, New Mexico, I always looked forward to the fiesta in September; people took to the streets in costumes and masks. I have seen men change themselves into tigers and wolves, and I know that masks only give a face to the deeper transformation that has already taken place. These chimeras, these monsters with human attributes, are very much a part of our own world. The mask annihilates you, as Rilke knew so well when he wrote:

Hot and angry, I rushed to the mirror and with difficulty watched through the mask the working of my hands. But for this the mirror had just been waiting. . . . While I strove in boundlessly increasing anguish to squeeze somehow out of my disguise, it forced me, by what means I do not know, to lift my eyes and imposed on me an image, no, a reality, a strange, unbelievable and monstrous reality, with which, against my will, I became permeated; for now the mirror was the stronger, and I was the mirror. I stared at this great, terrifying unknown before me, and it seemed to me appalling to be alone with him. But at the very moment I thought this, the worst befell. I lost all sense, I simply ceased to exist. For one second I had an indescribably painful and futile longing for myself, then there was only he: there was nothing but he.*

Put on a mask, and you put on another reality. The deadening repetition of habit—eating, sleeping, working—be-

* *The Notebooks of Malte Laurids Brigge* (New York: Norton), pp. 94-95.

comes the quickening repetition of ritual. The commonplace, particular acts that belong to no pattern and are rooted in necessity become symbolic acts. I light this candle and drink from this cup and break this bread because men have done so before me, and in doing these things once more I know myself to be part of the family of man. *"Take, eat, this is my body. And he took the cup and gave thanks, and gave it to them, saying, Drink ye all of it; for this is my blood of the New Testament, which is shed for many for the remission of sins."*

Shouldn't a worship service, then, make it easier for the worshiper to move from the commonplace level to the mysterious, symbolic level? The act itself is the same: you lift the cup to your lips as you would in a restaurant, you break the bread as you would in a friend's home. There you are not changed by these acts and you do them in nobody's name but your own. But in a service, these acts are more than themselves and you are more than a single soul moving across the face of the dark. To put you in touch with all those strangers who are really your brothers, I have written a service in which the audience wears masks. And if you should ever attend a performance of this service, I would tell you that my real aim is to make you take off the mask of yourself, one creature, and put on the mask of Christ, which includes all of us. But because this is so difficult, I shall be satisfied if you are able to take off your mask and look joyfully at man, who is never brighter than when he walks in the sun of love, where you can celebrate all his uncertainties and sorrows without fear, without judgment, without grief.

## A Wedding Masque for Lonely Travelers

*(Let all members of the audience be given masks to wear as they enter the church, theater, park, or meetinghouse. Let*

*there be a great variety of masks, some like animals, some like skulls of every color, some like the faces of strangers. Among the players, only the* BRIDE *and* GROOM *wear no masks.*)

MAN IN A BLUE SUIT (*With two candles in his hands and his cap under his arm, he steps before the audience*):

>You are all welcome here,
>you, soldier whose death feeds on my heart,
>you, thief who claws my throat for gold,
>you, old mother who sends me forth each day
>like a hawk and each night draws me back,
>and you, lovely one, dead so long
>yet always saying goodbye.

>If to marry means coming together,
>then I marry you to me and to each other.
>All those years I shut you out,
>you fattened yourselves on darkness.
>Now you touch me with tusks of pearl.
>I bless the dark pause between these candles.
>It makes them blaze.

>And every space between my words
>carries your praise.

(*He blows out the candles, puts on his conductor's cap.*)
All aboard!

(*Enter* DANCERS *and* MUSICIANS, BRIDE *and* GROOM. *The* GROOM *wears a helmet and a cartridge belt, and he carries a gun.*)

All aboard for houses, fields, navels, the Delphic Oracle, hot porridge, temples, treaties, the cross, the cry, the fiery promise, the new world! (*To the* GROOM.) You have too much baggage, Sir. The door to this country is narrower than the eye of a needle. Give me that helmet. (GROOM *takes off helmet.*) And that gun. (GROOM *hands over gun.*) And those cartridges. (GROOM *unbuckles belt.*) We'll auction them off. (*He takes a bell out of his pocket, rings it, and everyone gathers around him.*) What am I offered for this helmet?

DANCERS: A helmet! Look at that, a real antique! Where on earth did he get it? I haven't seen one in years.

MAN IN A BLUE SUIT: What am I offered for this helmet? It's in good condition. (*He taps it.*) You know, there were thousands of these things made and you can comb the battle fields and not find one. Helmets are getting scarcer than arrowheads. Who'll give me a dollar? One dollar, one one one one, who'll give me one? (*He holds it up.*) Use it for an umbrella, if you're a turtle.

(*The* DANCERS *and* MUSICIANS *laugh.*)

A MUSICIAN: One dollar!

MAN IN A BLUE SUIT: I hear one dollar. One, going on two, who'll give me two, two two two two, who'll give me two? Do I hear two? Two going once, two going twice. Sold to the man in the red boots for one dollar!

(*The* MUSICIAN *takes the helmet to one side and examines it.*)

MAN IN A BLUE SUIT: And now, what am I offered for this magnificent gun? (*The gun is not a real gun but a flute, which serves as a muzzle, to which a papier mâché handle has been attached.*) A hundred years ago, every household had one. This one is in remarkably fine shape. You could put roses in it; surprise your wife with a new bud-vase.

(*The* DANCERS *and* MUSICIANS *laugh.*)

A wedding present for the couple that has everything. (*More laughter.*) What am I offered for this gun?

A DANCER: Fifty cents.

MAN IN A BLUE SUIT: Fifty fifty fifty, make it one dollar. One one one, make it two. Got fifty, make it one, am I offered one dollar, do I hear one dollar?

SECOND MUSICIAN: One dollar!

MAN IN A BLUE SUIT: I hear one dollar. One one one one, make it two. Do I hear two? One once, one twice, sold to the young man in the cap and bells.

(*The two* MUSICIANS *get together and compare their bargains.*)

MAN IN A BLUE SUIT: And last of all, I have here a genuine cartridge belt. (*The cartridge belt is made of empty toilet-paper rolls, fastened in a row on a strip of cloth.*) You hardly see one of these with all the bullets intact. All sorts of ways to use a cartridge belt. Hang it on the Christmas tree. Hang it on the front door. Let's start the bidding at five dollars, ladies and gentlemen. This is a real find. Who'll offer me five dollars for this cartridge belt?

(*Pause.*)

A DANCER: Five dollars.

MAN IN A BLUE SUIT: I hear five dollars. Five and a half, five and a half, will anyone go five and a half? Half half half half, five and a half. Five and a half once, five and a half twice, sold to the fellow in the black robe. (*He hands him the cartridge belt.*) Be careful. This was once considered a dangerous weapon.

(*The two* MUSICIANS *play, the* FIRST *uses the helmet as a drum, the* SECOND *uses the gun as a flute. The* DANCERS *clap their hands.*)

GROOM (*sings*):

> If I were a raven, she'd follow me south,
> If I were a shell, she'd drink from my mouth,
> If I were a harvest, she'd give me her land.
> Because I'm a soldier I conquer the others,
> reborn with a rifle to slaughter my brothers,
> the eagles and sparrows that fed from my hand.
> If I were an eagle, I'd carry her crown.
> If I were a spider, I'd spin her a gown.
> If she'll be the ocean, I'll be the sail.

If I were a free man I'd marry on Sunday.

Because I'm a soldier they'll take me on Monday

to harvest the corpses or wither in jail.

(DANCER WITH CARTRIDGE BELT *puts the whole belt on his head, so that it hangs down on both sides of his face, like a judge's wig. He stands on a chair.*)

DANCER WITH CARTRIDGE BELT: Bring the prisoner forward. (*The* FIRST MUSICIAN *uses helmet as a drum. Two* DANCERS *in black bring the* GROOM *before the* DANCER WITH CARTRIDGE BELT.) You are accused of refusing to take the life of another in the service of your country. You know that this is a serious offense, punishable by a ten-thousand-dollar fine and up to five years in prison. Will the defense for the accused please step forward?

BRIDE: I am the defense.

MAN WITH CARTRIDGE BELT: And what have you to tell this court?

BRIDE: You need this man more than you know. He's a healer.

MAN WITH CARTRIDGE BELT: Are you asking for a deferment? It doesn't say on his papers that he's a doctor.

BRIDE: I didn't say a doctor. I said a healer. (*To audience.*) Didn't I?

MAN WITH CARTRIDGE BELT: There's no difference.

BRIDE: Oh, yes there is. A doctor has to study before he can cure you. And he has to write out a prescription. A healer only has to touch you.

MAN WITH CARTRIDGE BELT: And where did he do his internship?

BRIDE: On earth.

MAN WITH CARTRIDGE BELT: And what's his specialty?

BRIDE: Worn-out faces, last year's birds, the broken horns of unicorns, stars that have lost their balance, lovers' quarrels.

MAN WITH CARTRIDGE BELT: There's no deferment for healers.

BRIDE: He also heals men.

MAN WITH CARTRIDGE BELT: Why didn't you say so? Then he *is* a doctor!

BRIDE: No, he's a healer. I appeal to the jury. (*To audience.*) You heard me say it: a healer.

MAN WITH CARTRIDGE BELT: What are his degrees?

BRIDE: He hasn't any.

MAN WITH CARTRIDGE BELT: No degrees! And you expect me to believe he can heal people! (*To audience.*) Has anyone in this room been healed by the accused?

BRIDE: I have.

MAN WITH CARTRIDGE BELT: I don't believe it.

BRIDE (*to* MUSICIANS): Play me some music, so the judge will believe it. (*She sings.*)

> All hot and cold with fever,
> wrapped in her husband's coat,
> She said, "I see Saint Michael
> rowing my father's boat."

> Her husband the magician
> piled blankets on the bed.
> She said, "I see my mother,
> she's throwing me a thread."

> Her husband the magician
> canceled his matinees,
> And from his net he scattered
> a skein across her gaze.

> She said, "If I cross over
> this river, I shall die."
> He knelt and drank the river,
> he sucked the fever dry.

She said, "I see the sparrows
and plums of paradise."
Out of his hat he ordered
apples and doves and mice,

To rub against her hands,
wasting against the sheet.
She said, "I smell the planets,
they're burning at my feet,

And time is burning slowly,
a slowly blackening flower."
He danced upon the bedstead,
he sang upon the hour,

Dark as the nighttime hat
in which all tricks begin,
Which orders forth the sparrow
and calls it back again.

With bread and milk he wooed her,
ashes and weddings, sewed
together in his mutterings
as through the woods they rode

Beating the woods together
until he knew they'd won,
And felt upon his wrist
the tamed and hooded sun.

FIRST MUSICIAN (*sings*):

      He married you to sunlight,
      he married you to stars,
      He married you to loneliness
      behind the prison bars.

BRIDE (*sings*):

> If I can't touch his loneliness
> I'll sleep outside his door.
> They'll hire me as a kitchen maid
> to scrub the prison floor,
>
> And if he doesn't notice me,
> I'll wash the prisoners' clothes,
> And every time I iron them,
> I'll find the one I chose.
>
> If we don't meet in this world,
> I'll meet him in the next.
> Your knives are turning silver,
> your guns are being blessed.
>
> Your prison is a forest.
> He'll perch there like a dove
> and wear in every weather
> the ragged coat of love.

(BRIDE *and* GROOM *dance, as* MUSICIANS *play. The* DANCERS *join in, they tug the* MAN WITH THE CARTRIDGE BELT *off his chair and they all dance together.* GROOM *stops, claps his hands. Everyone is silent.*)

GROOM (*To audience*): Take off your masks. (DANCERS, MUSICIANS, *and* AUDIENCE *take off masks.*) And take hands. (*To audience*): Now there is no more loneliness for you.

(DANCERS *dance a formal round.*)

FIRST MUSICIAN (*sings*):

> The holy town where I was wed
> was quick as moss and green as the dead,
>
> and in that town a church was born
> with doors all ivory and horn,

and by those doors the young priest knelt
with peacock's crown and panther's pelt,

and through that door the peasants spilled
to bury those the soldiers killed.

Now through that door come woman and man.
See how the country blooms again!

(DANCERS *and* MUSICIANS *lead everyone out, singing. The
masque should be followed by a walk in the woods, if the wedding takes place in spring or summer and the weather is kind.*)

# WORSHIP: MARRIAGE
# OF HEAD AND HEART

## by Dominic L. Cirincione

*Dominic L. Cirincione, Research Associate at the Western Be-
havioral Sciences Institute in LaJolla, California, is a psycholo-
gist who has experimented extensively with forms of worship
for heightening personal involvement. His insistence that a
recovery of profound personal and interpersonal experience
in worship should be the primary goal of liturgical renewal
formed a third general position in the seminar alongside the
recovery of the sacred and celebration of the secular as appropriate goals. He felt somewhat lonely in the coffeehouse service.—*Ed.

WE CONSISTENTLY miss the mark in religious and sacred reforms when we are not aware of our uprootedness from the
ground of religious experience, from that which is most deeply
human, from the life source which alone can give energy and
vitality to a growth-change world.

As a nonprofessional theologian, but as one who has taken
religion and theology seriously all of his life, I have seen theologians much inclined to learning peering at contemporary
problems of religion, morality, and worship through micro-
scopes of scholarship and through telescopes of prophecy.
These viewpoints, although valuable to certain individuals and
in certain circles, are for the most part incomprehensible and
irrelevant to the majority of Christians.

Another viewpoint more commonly ensnaring and, therefore, more insidious, is the one that assumes God and his
world are really completed, defined, and, therefore, unchang-
ing—a picture quite pleasing to Aristotle. Yet human experience and insight as revealed through such thinkers as Albert
Einstein and Teilhard de Chardin indicate that God is emerging, is happening, is appearing and continually vitalizing our
existential reality. In this world-view, continuity, change, convergence, and emergence are not simply a possibility; they are
imperatives.

Personally, I cannot believe in or accept the static world-
view and that our present dilemma is one of historical in-
evitability. Rather, I see our chaotic, rebellious condition as
the result of polarization or schizophrenia, of the dichotomy
expressed in the alienation of feeling from action, in the
separation of eros and agape, and in the divorce between
Dionysus and Apollo. Intuition suggests that we must return
to the ground of our personal experience to regain the
wholeness of holiness. Only when we grasp what is basic, in-
trinsic, and fundamental in human experience can we touch
the transcendent force of our communal identity. This is the
binding force of Christian life and the source of living worship within which we feel the oneness of the body of Christ.


## Apollo's Apoplexy

I would like to dwell briefly on Apollo and Dionysus rather
than on the strictly religious and psychological polarities.
Apollo, the headstrong master of Western culture, was raised
in classical fashion under the tutelage of Greek reason, philosophical scholasticism, Protestant decency and order, and
American science and technology. Apollo has become our
teacher in turn and disciplined our minds in the categories of
Aristotle, our feelings in the courts of jurisprudence, and our

bodies in the pillory of reward and punishment. Apollo stands
for form and for the finite, for control and classical idealism.
Whereas Dionysus, Apollo's unruly brother, represents energy,
infinite dance, enthusiasm, and romantic revelry. The face of
Apollo is serious, for he must scrutinize right and wrong, administer order and discipline, guard sanity and civilization.
This face also masks a sadness and a longing for the lost twin
brother who enjoys the continuous open streams of human
contradictions and the pastures of pleasure, while Apollo remains rigid, reasonable, and removed. It is in the coming together of the two brothers that growth is ensured, for Dionysus must destroy one wall so that Apollo can build a better
one. But Dionysus without Apollo brings chaos, and Apollo
without Dionysus yields death and stagnation.

## Do Not Disturb, I'm Talking to God

Most of our contemporary worship is structured in the tradition of Apollonian wisdom. Everything from church design to
personal attitude (do not disturb, I'm talking to God), reflects
the removed and rigid stance of classical columns reaching
toward the sky. Well-carved and secured pews guard the aisle
to the holy place wherein the written word and the body of
Christ are sheltered and dispensed. Each pew defines a person's place, and places him under arrest until his hour of observation is over. A booklet or hymnal further separates him
from everyone around him while he is invited to rejoice and
celebrate the community of Christian brotherhood. The Sunday worshiper commemorates the history of Israel and the
Lord's Supper with bowed head and somber isolation, but
never is asked to celebrate the history of his own life and the
supper of his own pain and passion in the world.

With wayward attention, the Sunday observer listens to the
minister explain the word of God and to the exhortation to

personal action, "that the holiness of life may be made manifest in an unholy world." The peace is given in words and tones meant to encourage gladness, singleness of heart, and steadfastness. Steadfastness indeed! One needs to be steadfast as he plunges from his pew to face the parking-lot scramble, the Sunday drivers, and the delights of opposing interests at home. Perhaps the head has been touched at this Sunday service, but our body of personal, social, and economic disparity needs a heart to incarnate the joy of life, not another head to dictate to its unexpressed feelings and frustrated dreams.

William F. Lynch in his book *Christ and Apollo* speaks of Apollo in these terms: "Let him [Apollo] stand for a kind of autonomous and facile intellectualism, a Cartesianism that thinks form can be given to the world by the top of the head alone, without contact with the rest of the self." This illusion of separation of head from body has brought us to the arid, repetitious kind of questioning which cannot give rise to meaningful and alive forms of worship. To return to an earlier theme, the central one, it is only when the head is in the service of the body that the total organism can breathe creative change, and new life emerge.

If we take Christ's words seriously, that he came that we might have life and have it more abundantly, I think we can begin to appreciate that we must be in touch with our life source, which is dwelling within our bodies. It may be humiliating at this sophisticated point in history for man to accept that he is existentially grounded in flesh and blood and from this grounding arises his agony and his ecstasy. In a paper presented to the American Psychological Association (San Francisco, August, 1968), Stanley Keleman, a well-known bioenergetic therapist made this observation.

A person who has contact with his own body is in contact with his feelings, his drives, his own sensations, his own pleasure on many levels and can, at the same time, be in relationship with nature, feel part of nature, feel the sensations that emit from nature, is grounded, is healthier. When you are grounded, you understand that you are a body, you are flesh and blood. Sensations arise out of your body, you have sensations coming from nature, you can feel connected to the world, you feel connected to others and to yourself. A person who lives in his images, images that either deny his body or his body feelings or sensations or tries to reconstruct them in a way in which he rises above them is out of touch, is not grounded.

I am firmly convinced that it is in involvement with life's process and commitment to life's thrust that God is made manifest. If we are at one with ourselves, we can and will be in touch with and at one with others. In these terms, the mystical body of Christ lives and has its being.

This critique of the present condition of worship paints a bleak picture, but it does not seem to distort the truth that by and large our services are instructional and interpretative, predictable and pious, organizing us into a body which lacks a heart. Our communion is in the bread and in the cup, but our thoughts and feelings are not communicated. As one writer has put it, "One might think that sharing recognizable bread and drinking from a common cup would be dramatic enough, but history and habit can dull the brightest hue." The once deeply significant gestures become a detached mime, not a spontaneous action, but a muted stimulus with a mechanical response.

One final observation reflecting the state of affairs in a word-oriented worship concerns the homiletic hallucination that saying a word gives it substance. Words such as "involvement," "personal commitment," and "Christian participation" are being drained of their impact for lack of personal reference in the listener's life. These words are all expressions of dynamic activity and ways of being alive, but when used in the context of almost complete passivity, they leave the worshiper floundering at sea while trying to bridge the gaps between Sunday and Monday, sacred and secular, belief and unbelief, myth and mystery.

## The Canterbury Courtship

Today's experiments in worship seem to me to be an attempt at wedding to Apollo's rigor the rhythm of Dionysus' dance. This rhythm has not taken on the full zest of a nuptial feast, but rather resembles a courting ballet. I feel that this was true also of the Canterbury service. The coffeehouse is a forum for dramatic events of every variety. It is a place where the logic of political argument often collides with the warmth of deep emotions and poetic license—a fitting place for Apollo and Dionysus to meet.

The participants at this Sunday morning event gathered in clusters in the center of the floor and in rows along the walls. Physical isolation was not an obstacle as in a traditional church. The first juxtaposition to this casual, unstructured setting appeared in the form of the minister who was dressed in full ceremonial regalia and entered to rock music accompanied by electric guitars. The theme of journeying or pilgrimage was set by the opening song.

The first question which came to my mind was, Could we have in some way incorporated this theme of entering-in, of pilgrimage into a body experience, something felt through action? The entrance song and theme of entering into the house of the Lord would then have a personal grounding. As the community gathers, I would suggest that each two people select another pair and that these four choose two more, forming a micro-community who will remain a unit for the duration of most of the service. This small group could then spend a few minutes sharing their personal discoveries with one another. In addition to establishing a feeling of a corporate identity within the body of the church, such small groups might begin to restore the confessional element of worship in some meaningful way.

The parable called "Cranky" represented a good visualization of a son's journey into the pain of conflict and the desolation of separation. It was an epistle in some ways which focused our attention on an issue crucial to us as individuals and to the brotherhood of man. Yet it was not developed and directly related to the Old Testament reading, which was in harmony with the "Cranky" parable.

The prayers and readings that followed seemed to be linked thematically in only a shadowy way to what had occurred just before. My impression was that the readings arose more from a liturgical imperative than as a natural response to a happening. The openness of the setting, the contemporaneity of the music, the impact of the Mime Troupe were Dionysiac overtures to the Apollonian ritual, prayers, and vestments. There were moments of encounter, but a relationship was yet to emerge.

The exchange of the Peace and the recitation of the Creed heightened the paradox for me that we are one in some mystical sense, but not in an existential sensibility. The dichotomy between old words and new music, between old worlds and current problems, between traditional beliefs and present inquiry might be joined in the ground of common belief if the expression of our belief were not juxtaposed by words muted by repetition. We must present our living faith as the basis for our Christian dedication and creed. Perhaps some time could be given in the worship service, even replacing the homily on occasion, when the people could make some personal statements about what they believe in the concrete pursuit of their lives. An alternate community creed might be expressed in a dialogue between the minister and the congregation, focusing on what light in one's life leads to more loving function in his everyday life.

The prayer of intercession to my thinking was an opportune moment for the presentation of personal concerns and communal cares, either reflected in the reading of news headlines or in the personal petition of a participant. Instead, the general intercessions read seemed awkward to me because the here-and-now lives of those sitting on that coffeehouse floor did not relate to these categorical concerns.

The film at the offertory presented the community with a touching and sensitive experience of sound and sight, but no one offered his reactions as to what that beauty meant to him. This would have been a fitting participation which might have given each person an awareness of his individuality which becomes leaven in the bread of life.

From entrance hymn to offertory, the collage of events moved in rapid succession to the preparation for the consecration—the central action and symbol of the service. Perhaps it is at this very juncture that one noticed a lack of directionality and missed the feeling of a central moment approaching. To me this reflects in a deep way the lack of grounding in the mystery of life and love, a deficit which has brought us to a place of disconnected eclecticism in liturgical renewal.

The recitation of the *Sursum Corda,* the Preface, *Sanctus,* and *Benedictus* prayers, rich in historical significance and Christian aspiration, lacked inspiration at a time when it was most needed. The problem in simply verbalizing over and over again beautiful words without deepened awareness and conscious intentionality is that we are filled with sound but not sensation. I refer here to a statement made in a paper called "The Importance of Being Carnal—Notes for a Visceral Theology" by Sam Keen:

In order to arrive at the definitive saving act of God which is the source of grace, the existing individual must turn aside from (1) his immediate bodily sensations, (2) his involvement in nature, (3) his current cultural and political situation, and take a trip back into ancient Israel. Characteristically, Protestantism has declared that healing comes not from what may be seen, or felt, or touched, but from *hearing* the word of God. The ear is the organ of salvation. To the person whose ears are closed to hearing of God's mighty acts in the history of Israel, there can be no adequate understanding of grace.

If our ears are the organs of salvation, God has done us a great disservice in giving us other organs of sensation and perception. For it is in our total bodies that we feel the beauty and grandeur of grace and nature and appreciate the miracle of human love in all its gracefulness.

To return to the small groups, which I have neglected for some time, I would here envision latitude for sharing of gifts, aspirations, anxieties, and blessings. In some services, these could be done in verbal or nonverbal ways, in mime or in drama, in dance or in song. When we touch the heart, the expressions of love will be manifold. The word needs flesh really to dwell among us.

We now boldly say, "Our Father." It is bold, to my way of thinking, to say "Our Father," not because we are unworthy of God's love, for we are expressions of his love—but, rather, because all too often we do not act as if the person sitting next to us is our brother. If we are bold and presumptuous toward each other, in taking each other for granted, or in not giving ourselves unconditionally to others, we probably are acting in the same fashion toward our Father. "If any one says, 'I love God,' and hates his brother, he is a liar; for he who does not love his brother whom he has seen, cannot love God whom he has not seen" (1 John 4:20). So, in our prayer of brotherhood and mutual forgiveness, it seems fitting that we should turn to one another and make some personal statement of how I see you—the other—as my brother. The formal prayer could be said with everyone holding hands in a large family-chain reaching to and focused in the minister.

In administering the bread and wine to one another, as a symbol of the life-giving food of love, I felt a true unity of caring and a genuine humility of service in our worship. This human action touched on a central point of the Lord's Supper wherein Jesus laid aside his garments and served his brothers, not out of false humility, but out of humble respect: "For I have given you an example, that you also should do as I have done to you." This model of serving is paradoxically well taken in calling our worship a service. Yet how frugally we serve others and how reluctantly we share ourselves in this celebration of our love feast.

Here, at last, in giving bread and wine to one another was an opportunity to attend to and make contact with the person next to us as part of the liturgical action. It struck me that it was in the breaking of the bread that we began to know one another, which affected a true sense of community. The carryover of this communion was felt in the singing of a thanksgiving round.

My thought, as we left the coffeehouse, was, "Dionysus and Apollo have got a good thing going—but where to from here?"

## Conciliation Court

In our attempt to reconcile, reform, and renew worship for contemporary culture, I believe that the mediating ground must be the worshiping person. The churches in their central activity of offering worship to God must become places of convergence for the expression of man's search for meaning in the evolving mystery of life. Without this commitment to a personal central focus, our attempts at renewal will run the risk of becoming only reflections of an external world in which Christians remain observers, much like today's television viewers.

For a man to reach out to the transcendent God of the universe, he must begin by touching the unity of his own identity in community. It is precisely within the context of a person's own life—his microcosm; his past and his present —that the continuity of life's meaning arises and from which he creates his future and trusts in the ultimate meaning of the macrocosm.

Worship stands or falls depending on the ground's firmness. Thus the ground of worship is belief; this territory is by no means firm. The concept of belief or faith would cease to have meaning if it were static, defined, a closed-truth system. In and of itself faith means a continuance of striving, of promise, of at-one-ness, and of being in process with the developing, pulsating life of the world—in God's world, in his life, in his presence and expression.

It is in this world that we discover the roots, the streaming source of living faith, the phenomenon which has been called our religious experience. This is the encounter which turns a man around (*metanoina*), which turns him on (grace), which renders him open (humility), which gives him ecstasy in the *mysterium tremendum*. With such an energizing ground, we must offer space and time for persons to locate their roots in a cracked and heaving earth. For if liturgy does not grow out of belief and if belief does not spring from the source of man's life—his experience in the world—we relegate belief and worship to the Apollonian dungeon of the mind. I personally feel that this is to slight, undercut, and depersonalize the God of Israel, the God of Christianity, and *a fortiori* to do the same to man, his son and his likeness.

"Out of the depths we have cried to you, O Lord." And into our depths we must return to find the voice which longs for its body, love's body, the one body I call mine, the mystical body of oneness in Christ.

# SPONTANEITY IN WORSHIP

## by Gilbert H. Caldwell

*Gilbert H. Caldwell is District Superintendent of the Boston District of the Methodist Church. In the seminar discussion and in his paper, he, like Cirincione, is concerned with the recovery of personal involvement in worship, but his idea of "involvement" is less muted and interior, more robust and expansive than Cirincione's. As Caldwell says, he judges worship from his lifelong experience in the ecstatic and full-blooded tradition of the Black Church. He liked the direction the coffeehouse service was taking, but wished it would move toward its goal faster and in greater depth.*—ED.

I CAME TO the Ann Arbor experience as I come, and as most Black men come, to any event these days, asking certain questions and searching for the presence of Black people. The question I asked of myself: "What relevance do these moments of discussion and worship, in this predominantly white setting, have for me and what I call the Black Revolution?" "What experience can I have and what can my presence here do to speak to my brothers and sisters in Black communities all over this land who have seen no element of hope in the Church of Jesus Christ?" "Am I here because of who I am internally; or am I here because of what America

says I am because of my external experience?" "Am I the
token, the symbol, the 'house nigger' whose presence simply
completes the diversity of the group?"

But what of our worship together? It does not need to be
said that we are in the midst of a revolution in worship.
Main-stream (white) churchmen are attempting to not only
"stand in the gap," but to bridge the gap between the secular and the sacred, the young and the old, the traditional
and the contemporary.

Black churchmen are rediscovering the elements of joy,
hope, and vitality that always existed in their churches and,
for a time, which many of us ran away from. I found myself
participating in the Ann Arbor experience hoping to observe
and share in the worship revolution. To some degree, I believe I did!

The thought of a worship service in a coffeehouse con-
jures up certain images in one's mind before one begins.
One has the feeling that the mere decision to participate is
an indication of one's revolutionary nature. One goes to the
experience, the "happening," feeling *avant-garde,* arty, superior, and with the feeling that "boy, I am really where it's
at."

One pities "all the lonely people" in their sterile sanctu-
aries worshiping in their cold uncreative way. There is an
understanding of the lyrics of "Eleanor Rigsby" in a new
way. One has a new appreciation of Father McKenzie "writing a sermon that no one will hear."

There is an attitude problem that one takes to coffeehouse worship (or that I took) that pushes one close to
feeling "holier than thou." I suppose this is true because
it is a "growing-edge experience."

I found myself wondering about the conventionality of
an 11 A.M. time for worship. Perhaps the hour was our link
with the traditional? In the midst of the service it suddenly

struck me that the officiating priest wore his liturgical garb. There was a definite note of incongruity here, but then I myself was an illustration of this same incongruity. There I was seated on the floor in my Sunday best when I would have felt much better in something else. Ah, life is filled with contradictions!

But then the service itself—and I can best speak of it and to it by making some rambling and unconnected observations. Upon entering, there was an atmosphere of congeniality and conviviality that was important to me. People were there waiting for the Word to be given! They were "loose" enough not to worry about disturbing their neighbor who was engaged in solitary worship. I get a bit bothered by the bulletin notice that appears in some churches urging worshipers to keep their mouths shut so that they will not disturb their "praying neighbor." (ENTER IN SILENCE—DEPART TO SERVE.) If one cannot speak to his brother or sister before and in the midst of worship, how in the name of heaven is he going to serve him when he gets outside?

I noticed the "little things" and I shall leave to my more intellectually perceptive colleagues the opportunity to lift the profundities. The communion around the cups of coffee and doughnuts that preceded the beginning of the service impressed me. There was a contrast in this undirected Eucharist and the directed one that was a part of the service. I liked the way "the folk" seemed to really relish the doughnuts and coffee. They seemed to be hungry and thirsty and were not just imbibing and eating because it was socially acceptable. I now remember that the budgets and eating habits of collegians make any encounter with food a real experience!

Already the reader can see my biases emerging. I feel that there has been so much hypocrisy in our worship. We live out our lives as sensual men and women who are a combination of the emotional, rational, psychological, etc., but when it comes to worship we go into our "worship bag," put on our masks, and sing the "Gloria" with no feeling. We are real and alive in a football stadium whereas most of the time in worship settings we are cold and aloof. Hungry and thirsty people at our worship service who dared to feed their faces was a novelty, and I found this to be utterly refreshing.

The music in the background before the worship service created the atmosphere that made this before-worship Coffee Hour so great. Then came the beginning of worship and our mood shifted, for now we were to focus on the Eternal Mysteries of Life and we became, despite the setting, artificial and different people. Fortunately we were saved from developing the "traditional worship mood" by our worship leader who, in spite of his garb, was able to project a relaxed, cheerful, open, and sharing attitude among us.

The presence of the actors from the San Francisco Mime Troupe was important! What a great idea it is to include in the experience of worship the real "preachers" of our day: the actors, the musicians, the poets. Their presence in our midst, their ability through the projection of feeling and intensity to "hold us up against" the agony, the dying of the real world, was important to me. It was important for it was in this moment that I felt the involvement, the sense of joy and agony that I experience when I worship in the Black Church. I found myself wanting to cry, to cry out, to laugh, to participate as the actors through the artistry of pantomime reminded me of the world I am trying to help revolutionize and radicalize. They seemed to evoke a kind of spontaneity within us that was different from what we felt as we sang.

I rediscovered in Ann Arbor that no matter how unstructured the service, no matter how lusty the singing, no matter

how informal the setting, no matter how free folk feel—
white folk just can't break loose into the extemporaneous,
the unprogramed, the way Black folk can! Despite all the
trappings of creative nonstructure, inhibitions are there and
folks don't seem to be able to break away.

I predict that the survival of worship, the future of the
Christian Church, will be determined by how quickly we
are able to mesh the freedom and spontaneity of the Black
Church with the creativity and radicality of the young
White Church. Notice I say young White Church and I say
it because quite honestly what I saw in Ann Arbor makes
me far more willing to continue to be in conversation with
white churchmen than what I see in most local white
churches that I know about.

The Beatles' "Hey Jude" was another high moment in the
worship service for me. It was here that the worshipers
seemed to remember that they had brought their bodies and
instead of going through programed "swaying" the way we
did as we used to sing "We Shall Overcome," folk sort of
moved around in ways that were peculiar to their own God-
given particular nature. Some of us attempted to sing the
lyrics, others of us tried to squirm to the melody, and some
even went into "transcendental trances" mesmerized by
John Lennon and Company. There was joy in our response
that was to be contrasted with the sense of sorrow that was
present as we shared in the movements of the Mime Troupe.

I found the liturgy a bit meaningless in this setting. I
had the deep feeling that our liturgist had a Word for us
that was not heard because he was encased by the Liturgy.
Our worship forms, as well as our garb, have done such a
great job of concealing who we are and what we are about.

The Lord's Supper itself served from wine bottle to cup
was a real emancipating act for me as a Methodist District
Superintendent. I thought to myself, "Boy, if the old Tem-

perance boys could see me now." We all have our "hang-ups"
but, fortunately, I was free enough not to deprive myself of
the Lord's Supper because our liquid came from "fermented
grape" rather than from our Methodist "unfermented
grape." For the first time, I saw the Eucharist as a "toast"
to the Lord Jesus Christ and as an act of thanksgiving for
what God had done through Him, for the world and thus
for me. Would it not have been great if at this moment as
we raised our cups each of us could have made public our
own personal "toast" (testimony)?

I believe the Ann Arbor worship experience says a number of things:

1. The experimental quality present in our worship service
   is a must in order to maintain the kind of open-endedness
   and freedom necessary to worship in the second half of the
   twentieth century.
2. The presence of the members of the San Francisco Mime
   Troupe in the worship service not only provided a dramatic experience but held up before us the idea of drama
   in the context of worship. Their deliberate and intense
   portrayals make some of our lukewarm, insipid moments of
   worship look silly.
3. It is difficult for all of us who have been exposed to traditional worship patterns to make a transition to the kind
   of worship experience that incorporates our normal activities. I thought there might be dancing before, during, or
   after our service but for some reason the collegians sub-
   dued themselves. We must ask the question, At what point
   is it necessary for worship to transcend and thereby stifle
   our "normal" life style?
4. Finally, the Ann Arbor worship experience has provoked
   within me a desire to experiment in a number of different
   ways utilizing resources that come out of the Black Com-

munity. There is present within the Black life style this substance called "Soul." What a great experience we might have with James Brown, Aretha Franklin, LeRoi Jones, Lou Rawls, Sun Ra, and hundreds of others. The in-put these persons and their groups could make to a worship service is fantastic. Possibly another time we can bring together those who are products of the Black experience in America with those who are rebelling against the emptiness of the white experience and see what God might cause to happen.

# EMOTIONAL RESONANCE
# AND LIFE CHANGE IN WORSHIP

## by Tony Stoneburner

*Tony Stoneburner, poet, professor of English Literature at Denison University, and liturgical scholar, echoes fellow-Methodist Caldwell when he describes his expectations of worship: "It will have emotional resonance (dull occasions are not worship) and life-changing power (occasions in which one remains what one has been are not worship)." In his paper, he carefully tests the coffeehouse service against his McLuhanesque understanding of the new culture.—ED.*

IN OUR TIME, Christian worship has become more and more problematical. Faithful members find it empty or impotent. Marginal members find it phony. When this happens, I think that experimental worship is essential. Why is this so?

As culture changes, the Church preserves forms which emerged during previous periods of creativity. The Church retains the forms intact but the different cultural context blurs or hides the original meaning. Oddly enough, the more obscure the forms are, the more sacred they tend to become. Eventually the cultural lag is so great that there is a credibility gap and people either say that the Spirit does not speak or they say that He speaks to someone else. Then another outbreak of creativity occurs. The Church borrows forms from the growing edge of culture, and through them people hear the Spirit speak once more. The speech is colloquial and vernacular. The eucharistic bread is daily bread. Redeemed life is ordinary life. We see such movements of reformation with Francis of Assisi, Martin Luther, John Wesley, and the liturgical movement of the nineteenth and twentieth centuries. Today the Church once more finds itself faced with a credibility gap, and in that void seeks and waits for the Spirit again to erupt and speak healing.

As a Methodist, I lack a denominational theology of worship. If I have a theology of worship, it is personal and eclectic, and its elements do not fit together neatly and completely. But as a Methodist, I also carry within me two traditional expectations of a service: it will have emotional resonance (dull occasions are not worship) and life-changing power (occasions in which one remains what one has been are not worship).

Worship is communal in nature: each person has a part to play, just as each aspect of the person (corporeal, emotional, intellectual, social) has its part to play. As a result, worship is human fulfillment; it is the actualization of the total human potentiality for a community of love. It is dance and song and speech in a drama that re-presents the Christian story for encouragement and imitation.

The newly emergent factors in worship today can be glimpsed from the roll of the new types of participants: the death-of-God adherents, the demythologizers, and secular theologians; dropout hippies; annihilistic New Left revolutionaries; inhabitants of the global tribal village (as analyzed by McLuhan and Ong); conscious participants in the noosphere (as analyzed by Teilhard); those against interpretation (as analyzed by Sontag). Spokesmen for these groups cannot claim to do more than speak for their own groups, and yet they articulate a sense of actuality acknowledged as the experienced world by a much larger number of people. What they say hints at the present shape of authentic worship (that is, worship that correlates with our sense of actuality).

The death-of-God and demythologizing theologians shift the story from God-and-Jesus to Jesus-and-us. Worship is no longer re-presentation, re-enactment, or retelling (*anamnesis*). It no longer considers what God has done for us but what we can do for mankind (on the model of Jesus of Nazareth). Recital of the past gives way to projection of the future. Divine gift in Christ becomes human task (Christic life).

The secular theologians eradicate the distinction between the sacred and the profane. The claim that special times, places, languages, groupings, and activities are the characteristics of worship has lost its authority. People working and playing in the world are just as much God's people as those who are doing things in set-aside places of worship. Worship is no longer special and hidden, shut up in cubbyhole privacy; it is ordinary and exposed, out in the open main-street marketplaces. A service renders service. If a gathering does not achieve attitudinal-social change, it is not worship.

Authentic worship in our time, then, has the character of the Church in pilgrimage (as analyzed by R. Schwarz). Demonstrations for racial justice and international peace are the liturgies of unity, among Christians and within mankind: a demonstration actualizes in epitome the possibility demanded. Worship occurs when a group of persons recognizes something that needs righting in society (the New Left revolutionaries) or in the cosmos (Teilhard) and responds to correct it, or at least to enact symbolically the need to correct it in order to recruit support for the undertaking. Worship occurs only where the action is.

The hippies, on their side, call in question the goals and motives of our culture. They emphasize the spontaneous and the extemporaneous. *They* cannot program *now* and *you* cannot program *me*. Each person does his own thing.

There is total participation (McLuhan: everything at once instead of one thing at a time). Doing what the spirit moves one to do, as at a happening or a be-in, is authentic worship.

Although such behavior no doubt sounds like the chaos in the church at Corinth from which Paul recoiled, worship occurs only upon occasions in which one can make a personal contribution.

Worship enlarges awareness and illuminates existence. If we have to say what worship means, the implication is that the occasion is not interpreting us. Every explanation (either historical or psychological) which we have to make of congregational behavior during a service is an additional instance of not-being-spoken-to, of being-left-out-in-the-cold, of alienation. For worship occurs only upon occasions in which group behavior interprets group existence. Worship is our joyful and solemn working and playing to appropriate and approximate the story of Jesus of Nazareth in the world.

What elements, we may now ask, are essential to worship that is authentic? It excites and interests. It expresses the joy of life and concern for others. It changes persons. It is a brief, continuous, cooperative action. Everyone has a role to play and a contribution to make. Its meeting place is secular, functional, convenient. It combines a rigidity of overall structure with a freedom for variation and experiment within the individual constituent units. It bears the mark of its own time. There is a change of emphasis from recalling the past to projecting the future, from divine gift to human task. There is a change of emphasis from the visual to the aural and tactile and kinesthetic. The oral word reverberates and music rumbles. Dialogue and dance spring up. The body experiences restoration to itself. Electronic media extend the senses. There is a change of emphasis from "knowing by reflecting" to "knowing by participation." Things appear without labels.

Before examining to what extent these marks of contemporary authenticity were present or absent from the Canterbury coffeehouse service, let me say first that Canterbury House takes experiment seriously, plans hard for it, and invests rich resources in it. And if I go on to say (as I shall) that the service finally triumphed, but over itself and almost by accident, it is not because I think less effort is better.

On the authenticity of the service, I would make these points:

- It is clear that the coffeehouse service spoke more idiomatically and attractively to the students, teachers, clergymen, and housewives present than any standard service. All kinds of persons were there and had a good time. In their responses, they tried as hard as the planners. Yet it must be noted that the service had no systematic revision of language and other symbols along death-of-God or demythologizing lines, although there was maintained an equilibrium between traditional and secular symbols, especially in the folkhymns.

- There was little sense that the assembled company was going to perform any other cooperative task in society. Worship did not form a community within the larger community. The congregation was not a group under a common discipline for the reformation of society either by infiltration or by frontal attack.

- There was little sense that each person was to do his own thing. While things kept happening, people participated only when they were invited by the chairman who was quite obviously in charge. Everything (except, perhaps, the unfolding of the final thing) was pre-arranged, with little room for spontaneous participation.

- The meeting place for the service was appropriate, secular, functional, and convenient. Already a place of meeting to

eat, drink, talk, and otherwise enhance life, it seemed ideal
for the Eucharist, a happening for the celebration of the
presence and action of Jesus which is continuous with the
other happenings there.

- The service plainly showed the marks of its own time. Electronic media were everywhere. As we entered the room of
worship, it was booming and throbbing with the bombard-
ment of folkrock through loudspeakers from a three-man
combo (guitar, drums, doublebass). The table for the celebrant bristled with a wasp-swarm of stable stand-mikes.
The southeastern stageapron corner had a mobile hand-
mike. Liturgical and scriptural words issued from several
spots in the room. Especially suited to the phonic or sonic
was the reading of a rhyming passage of Job in Hebrew:
an action which would occur only in a culture sensitive to
sound and permissive of the phatic. Unfortunately, music
of voices did not rival music of combo. People did not
learn to sing the sung parts of the service very well. Although they sang the folkhymns wholeheartedly, they
sang them only somewhat better. They did sing well the
final five-part round. (Perhaps the music would have more
nearly furnished a vehicle for free and joyful expression
if it had been taught orally rather than "literately"—because sight-reading seems beyond most of us—and if people trained in the music ahead of time had been distrib-
uted, deaconlike, throughout the congregation to lead and
support the efforts of novices.)

Like a crown of thorns interwoven with a crown of glory,
a group of lights fastened to overhead pipes flooded the
table for the celebrant. The allegorical color film at the
offertory introduced a sense of lightness, joy, and freedom
in the midst of much that was earnest or even strained.

- Body had only a few moments of realization. The congregation floor-squatted foursquare the whole (long) service
with a single jack-in-the-box jump-up exception for the

creed. In fact, we floor-squatted until our legs went to sleep, our buttocks flattened, and floor became a pain in the ass.

The moment for body to realize itself came when we touched our neighbors and swayed together. Contact as encounter at the level of touch is significant in the New Testament both for healing and for "communion" (the right hand of fellowship; the laying on of hands; the kiss of peace). As a person at the end of a line or row, I didn't want to be a nonconductor, a dead end; I wanted not only to receive touch but also to bestow it, to pass it on. Bottle-passing and distribution of bread and wine expressed some of the same haptic and somatic dimensions of existence.

Body was hampered by "literature," a servicebook and loose sheets of mimeographed music kept hands full, and misemphasized learning music and following the service by the eyes rather than by the ears. Items supplied as aids to worship were, at least in part, handcuffing handicaps. An acoustical world deserves acoustical aids, and body in a pulsing room ought to be free to move to the heartbeat of the music.

Sitting had another negative effect. It dramatized the fact that the company was split-level. Those seated on the stage were in a superior position to those seated on the floor and looked down on them. There is no gain in bring-ing the altar, lectern, pulpit to the level of the people un-less all the people are on a single level. The object of bring-ing celebrants and acolytes to the same level as the people is to have an architectural-social symbol of unity. The stage, which was fine for the performance of the Mime Troupe on Saturday night, was dysfunctional, an actual and em-blematic impediment for the worship of the congregation on Sunday morning.

- McLuhan has suggested that as the book becomes less our major means of knowing, booklike structures will become less dominant in our experiences. The stage will be with-

out proscenium arch, the painting without frame. Action
will not have a single center. The service groped to achieve
this with its shifting center of attention: the west wall for
Mime Troupe uncranking of dark crayon line-drawings on
butcherpaper and for the offertory film; the table in the
middle area facing the stage for the celebrant in his color-
ful white-and-gold vestments (which, by contrast, made one
aware how conventionally most of the worshipers were
dressed, unlike the theatergoers the night before) and for
the large wicker baskets to receive the bread and for the
reader of the Gospel lesson and for the Mime Troupe to
perform its commentary on it; the southeastern stageapron
corner for the huddle of conspiratorial assistants, includ-
ing the black-clad white-collared Fiji-haired chaplain and
filmmaker (Craig Hammond) who prompted reader of Old
Testament lesson and student leaders in prayer and himself read the Epistle lesson; the north wall between stage
and kitchen for combo. The four temporary centers dotted
diagonally southwest to northeast across the room. Slight
headturn and least hamshift brought each new center into
focus. Yet there was too little spatial or temporal shaping
of the congregation, which remained on the edge of being
a crowd, the verge of being a mass. The outline of the
order was lost like the skeleton of a mastodon sunk in a bog.

A former teacher and friend of mine, who had already
been to a Canterbury House service, predicted that the
service would start late and be haphazard but that Father
Burke would be at ease in presiding and guide the service
with dignity. My friend was proved right on all counts and
particularly about the adroit, almost casual leadership of
Chaplain Burke, his ad lib comments, and the dialogue he
would establish at points with the congregation. Some examples:

When explaining that there were not enough copies of

some music to go around, he summed up the situation with the comment, "The name of the game is sharing."

At the Peace he first chided the congregation for its timidity in touching and hesitation in swaying, then took the combo to task for not providing better music with which to move. The combo leader remained mum, and the trio merely doggedly finished the piece.

At the Prayer of Intercession when from the ambush of a prospector's beard the question came, "Why is prayer such a downer?" Chaplain Burke made the question more specific, "Why the unity of all Christian people rather than the unity of all people?"

At the end of the offertory film when a child asked, "Is there any more?" Dan quipped, "We could run it backwards."

At another point, he observed, "The thing is this: you're going to have to do it yourselves."

In fact, if all of us had been as alert and relaxed as Chaplain Burke, there would have been deeper dialogue, and an informality that didn't bog down. Chaplain Burke was cool, a man for the McLuhan world.

• The only thing wrong with the late beginning was that it hinted ahead of time that the service would last long. If the service of Holy Communion is to be a brief, concerted, continuous action culminating in communing, then each element, item, or unit should be kept as simple as possible. In the coffeehouse service there was no multiplication of the number of units. But there was an elaboration, embroidery, or expansion of individual units, especially of those for which a substitution was made (the three Mime Troupe items; the Old Testament lesson in both Hebrew and English; the film). Each of these tended to become something in itself. In its semi-autonomy, each was not so much a part of the ongoing main event as an interesting and worthwhile sideshow. We often lacked a sense of forward thrust gathering up separate items into a transforming totality. Thus, the relatively leisurely pace obscured the shape of the liturgy.

- The congregation was expectant, receptive, and most of the time responsive when given something to respond to. It could not be described as a congregation contributing, creative, extempore, improvisatory, spontaneous. The breakthrough came at the end, just at the point of commissioning dismissal (if one had retained a sense of the shape of the liturgy), when what at the time appeared to be almost a last-moment afterthought, turned out to be resolution and climax.

- The Mime Troupe did three things in the service. Against the west wall a small group uncranked their "comic strip" about a soldier going to Vietnam and accompanied it with a narration in basic English while a tune on a recorder fluted the distance between pastoral idyll and industrialized warfare.

In place of exegesis, homily, or sermon after the Gospel lesson read by Gil Caldwell (which ended something like this: "the people marveled that God had entrusted such powers to men"), this group mimed murder in the tiny cleared space. Four men in blue jeans and headbands rose, swayed, and circled while a voice over the loudspeaker read an account of the draft-records-destroying actions by the Catonsville Nine.

Eventually the voice fades and the rest of the presentation occurs in silence. One of the four men turns hitter. With his fist he fells the other three to the floor and then glories in his prowess by rippling his muscles and luxuriates in his victory. Two women, toting a bucket and a sheet for wound-dressing and corpse-shrouding, appear. The victor knocks one of them to the floor. The other one covers the now high-piled body-heap with the sheet. Then she dissembles admiration and affection for the self-congratulating victor, only to choke him to death with his loosened headband. As the avenger rises from the fallen body, she is panting and shaken. When her breathing gradually returns to its regular rhythm, she walks away slowly (as she did so, I thought about those women in the history of the Jews who defended their defeated people by acts of assassination) and the celebrant says, "On the night in which he was betrayed . . . ."

War-protest is appropriate to the Eucharist. Even so, nothing in the presentation indicated a change of relationship to "audience," to "congregation," on the part of the performers.

- The congregation turned on completely for the first time in the service only when, at the point of dismissal, the Mime Troupe performed a rendition of a five-part round. The congregation immediately showed enthusiasm for the performance, and the group taught the wordless music to us and led us in a congregational singing of it. We enjoyed it so much that we did not want to stop, in part because we liked not only the resultant sound (our most solid of the morning) but also the fact that it was of our making, and in part because it suddenly established a rapport between the Mime Troupe and the congregation which overcame the almost systematic pie-in-the-face audience-alienation of their theater: instead, there was the exchange between teachers and students, and mutual delight. At least a symbolizing of reconciliation had occurred. It was a triumphant event and more significant than their performance Saturday night and more significant than the rest of the Eucharist Sunday morning, except to the extent that the rest of it prepared for the breakthrough into rapport.

As emphasis on conversion in early Methodism changed the shape of the service and made the sermon secondary, so did emphasis on round-singing in the coffeehouse service make communing secondary and reconciliation primary.